California in the Balance

California in the Balance:
Why Budgets Matter

John Decker

2009
Berkeley Public Policy Press
Institute of Governmental Studies
University of California, Berkeley

Library of Congress Cataloging-in-Publication Data

Decker, John.
  California in the balance : why budgets matter / John Decker.
    p. cm.
  ISBN 978-0-87772-433-9
  1. Budget—California. 2. Fiscal policy—California. I. Title.
  HJ2053.C2D43 2009
  336.794—dc22

                                                            2009020655

To Anne,
For her continual kindness, and
In gratitude for an unwearied care,
A confidence which did not waver, and
Prompt succor in times of trial.

Contents

Foreword

Augury is not dead. Long ago, public officials consulted oracles about how to govern. Priests scrutinized the entrails of recently deceased birds and mammals to inspire their analysis. Their mysterious divinations could comfort and calm by judging the present and predicting the future, or simply by confirming the rulers' prevailing prejudices.

In much the same way, immediately after California's 2009 statewide election, news columnists went to work reading the entrails of California's election, interpreting the results with solemn certainty, and offering a variety of policy prescriptions and predictions about the state's fate. For example, *The Wall Street Journal* used the results to justify its call for repeal of the state's progressive tax system in the week after the election. *The Washington Post*, apparently using its own innards-analysis standard for distinguishing between the righteous and the unclean, declared that banks and car companies ought to receive federal financial assistance, but California was beyond the bail-out pale. It concluded that California had simply lived and governed itself unworthily for too long.

The foreign press was even more lavish in expressing disapproval. After examining the election results, *The Financial Times* decided that California ought to suffer the consequences of its actions, and thereby serve as an example for other profligate governments. *London Times* columnist Chris Ayers went further, and declared the state anathema, an outcast: "done, dead, . . . an ex-state. . . ." One can almost smell the sacrificial fires burning.

But are the modern oracles reading the signs properly? Will the giant sinkhole in California's budget swallow the state in short order, or will California somehow climb out of the financial abyss and back into the sunlight?

Finding the way through and beyond California's profound budget problems requires an understanding of the path the state has taken, year-by-year, decision-by- (well-intended-but-fateful) decision, to arrive at the brink. John Decker has undertaken to be our guide for a clear, thorough, and fascinating review of the succession of compromises, close calls, sidesteps, half-measures, and short-term expediencies that summarize California's budget and policy planning over the last two decades. Decker also shows us why many of those decisions were entirely unavoidable, analyzing the accumulation of policy barnacles added over the years to California's constitution by the voters through special interest initiatives and legislative ballot proposals that have so constricted the ability of California to navigate through hard times, much less to chart a course for the future.

As a long-time observer and sometime participant in California's budget-making process, I am not troubled when the state runs an occasional operating deficit. It has done so many times throughout its history without causing irreversible decline. In fact, during troughs of an economic cycle—when revenues fall faster than expenditures—it is generally considered fiscally prudent to run a short-term operating deficit. If the tax structure is sufficient to cover all expenses over *an entire business cycle*, then occasional recession-induced deficits can be financed during better economic times.

I am alarmed, however, by California's recent budget history. I have watched with increasing apprehension as:

1. Services degrade. Budget after recent budget, essential services have been cut. This continuing retreat from support for the aged and the vulnerable among our neighbors is discouraging and unfortunate. In the most recent budget, the state has cut dental services and incontinence supplies and palliatives to the state's poorest senior citizens. These types of cuts were unconscionable and unacceptable to Republicans and Democrats alike a generation ago.

2. Investments erode. Recent budgets have eliminated funding for maintenance of the state's capital assets, including parks, roads, and structures. Time-sensitive investments in critical capital projects, including schools and universities, have been deferred repeatedly. How can we explain to our children the failure to protect our assets and make timely investments?

3. Costs of service shift to "users." Basic services, once supported by the general taxpayer, have been shifted to "user-pay" schemes. There are certainly instances where the user-fee approach is appropriate and fair, but too often, when we shift costs from the general taxpayer we also diminish public confidence in the state's capacity and willingness to provide necessary services. User-pay schemes can tear the fabric of government services and erode the important sense of civic "ownership."

When did our budgeting practices begin to betray us? For me, two dates stand out as particularly fateful for California's finances.

Beware the Ides of July

In 1979, a legislative conference committee chose between two responses to the fiscal pressures created by the passage of Proposition 13. One response, proposed by Governor Jerry Brown, gave local governments the authority to impose a local sales tax. If enacted, the legislation would have let local governments retain threatened services *if they agreed to pay for them*. The other response, favored by the Assembly legislative leadership, shifted state revenue to cities, counties, and special districts. In this response, local governments could fund 90 percent of their pre-Proposition 13 spending *without raising taxes*. By July 15, the committee chose the state shift, which the *Los Angeles Times* lauded as the better alternative because it "permanently plug[ged] holes left in local government budgets."

The shift may have filled the budget "holes," but the bailout compromised the integrity of the state's fiscal structure. By choosing to use state revenues to backfill voter-approved tax cuts, the legislature gave taxpayers the false hope that they could cut taxes and maintain most of the services they had enjoyed before approving Proposition 13. Thirty years later, taxpayers continue to cling to this hope, even as the state veers from one unbalanced budget to the next.

Services must be financed. Want to fund an adequate school system? It must be paid for. Want a reliable safety net? Welfare workers must be paid and assistance checks can't be allowed to bounce because of insufficient funds.

Filling the local "holes" also led to a new and dangerous fiscal dependency. With the state bailout, local governments spent revenue derived from taxes levied by the state rather than from their own sources. Their ability to finance local services is a function of the state's fiscal condition. In good years, they can expect generous revenue sharing. When the state faces fiscal problems they are guaranteed a "share of the pain." No matter how the locals try to break this dependency, they remain subject to the ups and downs of the state's budget condition.

I concur with John Decker when he says that another key date must be Tuesday, February 18, 1992, when a handful of staff representing the legislative leadership and governor met informally and off-the-record to discuss how to close that year's deficit. They met in a decrepit state office building across the street from the State Capitol in the hope of finding a quick consensus budget fix. There, over a dinner of Chinese take-out, as the conversation circled the table, some wondered if the state could shift property tax revenue from local governments to K-12 schools. As the state General Fund would benefit on a dollar-for-dollar basis for every property tax dollar shifted, the proposal would allow the state to balance its budget without raising taxes or cutting programs. One of the Assembly staff, Sam Yockey (who later became Mayor Willie Brown's budget director), declared the idea the dumbest thing he'd heard: Why would the state want to insert cities, counties, and mosquito districts into the middle of the state's fiscal problem?

But the idea persisted. Governor Wilson inserted it in his "April Revision," and it has been a part of the budget ever since. The shift was explained as the "perfect" budget solution for the state, even as the maneuver reduced local discretionary resources. As a result, local governing boards, rather than the state legislature and governor, had to finance the deficit by closing libraries, restricting services, and raising taxes.

Expedience Drives Out Prudence

That 1992 meeting in a grubby upstairs conference room at 1020 N Street helped set a pattern for how the state has constructed its budgets in the years since. By relying on more arcane and obscure financing schemes, the legislature and a succession of governors have diminished anyone's ability to understand the complexity of budget decisions or to assess the fiscal tradeoffs.

In many ways, the state's experience parallels the crash of the Wall Street titans in 2007 and 2008. Just as few people on the planet understood the struc-

tured investment vehicles created by Wall Street's wizards, few Californians can
track how programs are funded or measure their performance. Budget decisions
operate in an alternate universe free from the weight of a logic or accountability
we mere mortals can fathom.

It would be one thing if the current process produced sound budgets, but the
results of this other-worldly decision-making has not served the state well. In a
world with compromised integrity, unhealthy dependence, and black-box solutions, budget choices reflect expediency instead of long-term good sense. It
seems that a successful budget is not measured by whether the fiscal plan is
"prudent," or even "balanced." Instead, a budget plan is deemed "successful"
when it can be described as "clever" or "painless."

It is not surprising, then, that California has consistently run operating deficits over the last 10 years, even during periods of relative economic prosperity.
Such a persistent mismatch is worrisome and difficult to justify.

When I became state treasurer, I was concerned about the state's ability to
finance its debt and plan for the infrastructure needs of a fast-growing state. I
asked staff to estimate the state's long-term fiscal condition, assuming a full-
employment economy. After running the numbers, they determined that the state
would, on average spend between 3.0 and 4.0 percent more than it takes in during each of the next 20 or so years. That is not a sustainable budget, but the good
news was and still is that a solution ought to be readily achievable as soon as
policymakers focus genuine attention to the matter.

At the time, I was confident that the state could begin taking action to provide for a long-term balance. The problem, which had developed over time, did
not require an overnight solution, provided that the legislature and governor
were serious about fixing the problem. Still, before the accounts could get into
balance the state would have to raise annual taxes, cut major services by billions
of dollars, or use a combination of both to set a new and balanced baseline. Two
years later, at the height of the worst global financial crisis of our lifetimes, the
immediate problem seems much worse than it did when we made those "best-
case" estimates.

Nevertheless, I am optimistic about California's future, unlike some of our
modern soothsayers. The state remains an inspiration and a destination for millions who understand California's promise—sometimes better than its leaders
do. California is a big, diverse state on the Pacific Rim. It is wonderfully situ-
ated to prosper in the coming years. It is generally more tolerant, more innovative, and better educated than other states or countries (though we have much to
do to ensure we continue to provide a good education to everyone). I believe the
future is brighter for our children and for all of us. To realize this brighter future,
we must encourage a strong and functioning public sector that emphasizes innovation, investment and transparency.

To protect our future, we must address our deteriorating fiscal condition.
We can do better, and by providing in this book an accurate, useful, and very
readable depiction of California state government's revenue and spending appa-

ratus and financial decision-making system, its rationale, and recent history, John Decker is donating to all of us a very valuable basis for reconstructing, revitalizing, and "rebooting" California's budgeting and financing process. That is a gift not only to California, but to a nation and global economy that badly needs the restoration of a prosperous, smart, and agile California to assure their own future success.

Bill Lockyer
State Treasurer
July 1, 2009

Acknowledgments

Few walk alone. To those who guided me on this book's path, I am grateful for having such companionable travelers. At the Institute of Governmental Studies, Jerry Lubenow and Ethan Rarick were considerate, generous, and patient editors. They gave ready encouragement and guidance. Maria Wolf, senior editor at IGS Press, with grace and charm formed the manuscript into this publication. Thanks, too, to Bruce Cain and Jack Citrin for supporting this project through to its completion.

Also at the University of California, Rob Gunnison and Susan Rasky, faculty at the Journalism School, taught me how to care for and extend a narrative. They gave freely their suggestions and encouragement.

John Ellwood, professor at the Goldman School of Public Policy, generously shared his budgeting class. With subtlety, he suggested research possibilities and direction. From our students in those classes, I learnt much about how the state ought to budget.

The university association I owe to Patrick (Please Don't Call Me Senator) Johnston. He is a great friend and mentor.

Sumi Sousa lent her apartment and kind words so that I might write in relative calm, while Rick Battson extended an open hand at critical times. Laura Doll, Peter Schrag, and Liz Kersten generously supported and advised me when this project began. Later help came from the staff at the California Debt and Investment Advisory Commission. I appreciate their help.

I could not have developed this work without the generosity of the Rocke feller Foundation. The manuscript came together during a research fellowship at the foundation's Bellagio Center on Lake Como. I am grateful to the foundation and Pilar Palacia, the center's director, for timely support, space to think, and the environment to write in uninterrupted days. While at the center, I benefited enormously from the consideration and friendship of Paul Sniderman and Paul Spickard.

My understanding of the state budget formed while working directly for many of Sacramento's talented leaders, including Senators Steve Peace, Wes Chesbro, Carole Migden, and Kevin Murray. On the Assembly side, they were Assemblymember Fred Keeley, and Speakers Antonio Villaragiosa and Bob Hertzberg. I am grateful to Assemblymember Phil Isenberg. In those Capitol years, I learnt much from fellow staff, especially Sam Yockey, Steve Olsen, Cliff Berg, Karen French, Tim Gage, Tom Hayes, Dennis Hordyk, Andy Meyers, Ellen Moratti, Chuck Pattillo, Fred Silva, Jo-Ann Slinkard, Peter Schaafsma, Greg Schmidt, Steve Thompson, and Brad Williams. All left a lasting impression. Their insights are evidenced throughout these pages.

Two years ago, State Treasurer Bill Lockyer appointed me executive director of the debt and investment advisory commission. He and Chief Deputy State Treasurer Steve Coony have been lavish in their support, providing boundless opportunities to teach and research on the state's debt and fiscal management consistent with the commission's responsibilities. Their generosity has made the difference.

Inspiration for these pages came from two people. And I can never fully discharge my debt to them. Senator Ken Maddy, who taught me to negotiate budgets, inspired with his unwavering belief in the importance of protecting the state's fiscal structure. By sharing her joy, care, and strength throughout these five years, Anne Maitland made this book possible.

Budgeting as Governing

The state's budget is a summary of expenditures for a surprisingly wide array of services. The range defies facile description, as it includes funding for kindergarten classes and campsites, healthcare for retirees and highway lanes reserved for commuting carpoolers. The political leadership of the state—the governor and Legislature—devote much of their time to formulating and negotiating an annual budget compromise.

In 2007–08, the state spent roughly $8.6 billion from the General Fund each month, or $7.48 per person daily.[1] The budget approved by the Legislature and governor affects every Californian every day. Given the broad impact of the budget, it is not surprising Californians have formed opinions about it. What is surprising is the level of discontent. Likely voters have consistently told pollsters at the Public Policy Institute of California that they see the state budget a "big problem." For example, in a 2008 statewide poll[2] about the budget, the institute found that 90 percent of Californians reported a "negative" perception of the state budget. Why?

Often, the barometer of success for these efforts is whether the budget is "balanced." By this measure, successful budgeting is an act of accounting; fiscal "health" deteriorates when the state spends more than it takes in. In reality, the budget balance is not a reliable measure of the state's fiscal condition. In recent years, through a series of off-budget transactions, over-optimistic assumptions and

---

[1] Department of Finance, Schedule 6, *Governor's Budget Summary 2009.*
[2] Mark Baldassare, Dean Bonner, Jennifer Paluch and Sonja Petek, PPIC Statewide Survey: Californians and Their Government. (San Francisco, Calif.) August 2008, 17.

questionable and unprecedented borrowing, the state's fiscal accounting system has been used to mask huge budget deficits.

Budgeting is more than measuring revenues and expenditures. Californians have learned that even a "balanced" budget does not ensure a "sound" or "prudent" budget. So, the budget takes on more meaning than a mere accounting exercise, or even a measure of fiscal health.

Each year, the Legislature and governor engage in successive rounds of political posturing and compromise as they develop the next spending plan. Because the governor and Legislature consider each budget on a set and annual schedule, their deliberations take on a ritualistic quality. Beginning immediately after the New Year holiday, the governor's press office "leaks" newsworthy aspects of the forthcoming budget proposal to those Sacramento-based reporters looking for copy during the slow news days at the start of the year. With these leaks, the governor attempts to shape the news about the budget to his advantage. In 2006, for example, Governor Schwarzenegger emphasized the need for financing capital improvements, both to advance his proposals for higher debt loads but also to distract attention from the growing operating deficit.

In the second week of January, the governor delivers the State of the State speech to a joint meeting of senators and Assembly members. In this forum—perhaps basking in the grandeur of the Assembly's ornate chamber—the governor shares a vision for the state's future. The governor also uses the speech to anticipate and blunt objections to the upcoming budget proposal. Later in the week, the governor calls a press conference to discuss, sometimes in excruciating and mind-numbing detail, his budget proposal. At the conference, which often attracts scores of reporters, the governor and the state's director of finance assess the state's general fiscal health. After the conference the Department of Finance releases thousands of pages detailing the governor's proposal.

It takes time to digest and assess all this information. Each house of the Legislature conducts an extensive review of the proposal. During a three-month period starting in March, the Legislature begins its line-by-line public review of the governor's proposals, while evaluating which proposals to adopt or to amend.

Every week during these months, each house holds four days of long committee meetings to review and take testimony about the smallest detail in the governor's budget. To conduct this review, each house's budget committee has a large number of members. At least one-third of the legislative membership sits on the budget committee. The budget committee staffs are the largest of any committee. The Legislature also funds an independent budget oversight committee, known as the Legislative Analyst's Office, to supplement the work of the budget committees.

During this portion of the legislative budget process, the public has wide access to information. For almost three months each year, members of the public may consider, along with each house of the Legislature, the governor's budget in minute detail. Californians can lobby to express their views directly. They may even testify before members of each house about the proposed budget.

In June, legislative leadership and the governor generally meet behind closed doors to develop a compromise proposal that the governor and Legislature can jointly adopt, typically sometime after July 1. Despite the well-articulated process by which it is developed and the extensive effort devoted to legislative consideration, the Legislature's budget product lends itself to time-honored and well-rehearsed hand-wringing about the adequacies of the adopted budget. Each year, Californians will hear that too much spending is lavished on ill-conceived and poorly administered programs. Certain programs, perhaps medical-assistance programs and "pork barrel" projects, are said to be wasteful or wracked by fraud. Then, Californians will hear that the Legislature failed to fund adequately essential government programs, like schools. From most commentators, they will hear that spending would be more "effective" if only the Legislature had the "right priorities."

When discussing the state's tax load, inevitably Californians will hear the complaint that taxes are too high and unfairly burdensome. At the same time, Californians will hear that someone is paying too little tax or not paying an appropriate share. They will hear that the tax system is designed to reward scofflaws and punish the honest. Of course, in the debate "scofflaw" and "honest" take on different meanings depending on the political perspective of the commentator.

They will hear that the process does not serve California's interests. Some will say that the majority party "rigs" the review process to prevent a fair debate on spending priorities, while others will say that the two thirds vote requirement "rewards" the prejudices of an uncaring minority. Budget delays and problems will, in this way, manifest political opinions.

One of the more popular ways to monitor budget developments is to track delays in passing the annual spending plan. A budget passed on or near the constitutional deadline is deemed "better" than a later budget. Delays into late August signify failure and inadequacy. Timeliness, in this way, is used to measure the political or pragmatic acumen of the state's top political leadership.

More than a barometer of fiscal health, the conduct and outcome of budget deliberations have become a proxy for assessing the quality of the state's political leadership. The schools disappoint because elected officials do not provide adequate funding for the right kinds of educational programs. The roads are crowded because the state's leadership neither properly plans nor finances adequately the freeways. Californians fear that politicians in Sacramento fail to address truly important concerns, such as providing adequate facilities at prisons.

Can There Be Change?

Given the institutional rules governing its passage, the annual budget document reflects a compromise developed between the Legislature and the governor. To the extent that this compromise gives substance to the diverse opinions in the state, the budget process could be deemed to have fulfilled its design and promise. The deep political divisions over fiscal policy that delay budgets and tend to heighten political acrimony are evidence of a fractured political consensus. If Californians have an innate suspicion of political compromises, perhaps their derision of the budget process and product reflects how deeply divided they are about the current and future direction of the state. Consensus budgets require broad agreements on the level of spending and the adequacy of the tax structure. Until a broad and sustainable consensus is found, is there a way to address the "negativism" identified by pollsters?

In the last 10 years, there has been no shortage of studies detailing the problems and possible changes, inevitably referred to as "reforms." Often, the solutions proposed have been tried, as evidenced by the number of initiatives placed before the voters to "fix" the budget or budget process. These "reforms" take the form of procedural changes: Increase the governor's power to make unilateral spending decisions, require greater fiscal austerity by funding "rainy day funds," or require specific funding of programs. Reduce the vote threshold for approving bonds from 67 percent to 55 percent. After these changes are made, the rituals remain mostly unchanged. The outcomes are vaguely alike. The complaints remain.

California's fiscal problems are unlikely to be changed by revising budget procedures. The process itself does not prohibit finding a stable and suitable solution. Rather, solutions elude the grasp of the state's leadership as it is difficult to simultaneously keep taxes low and generate sufficient revenue to cover all the state's spending commitments.

The state's fiscal problems have been persistent through three governorships. Confidence in the state has dropped to the point where large banks and money funds may begin to shun the state. After the budget passed in September 2008, the state treasurer fretted publicly about whether institutional investors would make short-term loans to the state, even at historically high interest rates.

Budget repair remains elusive. As Samuel Johnson dismissed Shakespeare's *Cymbeline* as having "faults too evident for detection," so many Californians can make the same complaint about their state's budget. To repair confidence, Californians will benefit from a better understanding of the competing demands on state spending imperatives and revenue structures. In this way, the challenges of constructing a budget suitable to achieve broad-based support will become more apparent. This book reviews the state's fiscal institutions and its budget troubles. It places the state's fiscal condition into its historical context, reviews the legislative budget process, and considers ways the budget fails the state. Upon this assessment, certain recommended changes emerge.

Chapter 1

Managing Conflict

For all its human limitations, California state government accomplishes something remarkable every year: It passes a budget distributing over $100 billion of General Fund revenue. Taking into consideration earmarked revenues, the budget allocates over $140 billion each year. These amounts represent $3,800 per person. Though the Legislature and the governor engage in long, often rancorous, public debates about fiscal policy, they agree to a spending plan every year. Their accomplishment, though easily dismissed as a mere accounting exercise, reflects considerable political acumen, effort, and compromise.

The Legislature and governor do not idle on the budget, patiently waiting for an opportune time to consider a spending package. To pass a budget, the principal parties must follow a structured and formal course of proposal and counterproposal. Often too, they engage in informal negotiations, which begin when the governor proposes his budget in the second week of January and continue at least through June and often through August. In 2008, negotiations continued through September. During these months, conflict around budget development and choices is "endemic."[1] Though California is not unique, the state's budget deliberations have become particularly divisive. In most years for California, the most obvious conflict follows partisan lines, as legislative Republicans generally advocate for reductions in spending and taxes. Democrats have tended to resist these cuts.

But other differences abound. They can be seen in each legislative caucus and between the houses. One house of the Legislature may develop and pass its budget proposal independently of the other. In late June 2002 for example, after working

---

[1] Irene S. Rubin, "Understanding the Role of Conflict in Budgeting," in *Handbook of Government Budgeting*, ed. Roy T. Meyers (San Francisco: Jossey-Bass, 1999), 30.

jointly on a budget solution, the two houses were unable to close on a final budget compromise. The Senate then passed a budget to the Assembly without further negotiations. The Assembly would not approve the Senate-only plan, and the state budget languished for two months past the start of the budget year. When the Assembly offered a counter-proposal in late August the houses could restart their negotiations to generate a compromise. In that year, the final budget passed on September 1.

Within the administration, department heads and governor's staff wrangle over which programs should be expanded and which strategy should be pursued for securing passage of important executive initiatives. Amid much fanfare the year after his election, Governor Schwarzenegger announced the results of a year-long internal effort to find efficiencies in government, known as the California Performance Review. Though most of the recommendations made in the review could be implemented administratively, few were actually taken in the form proposed. The failure to implement the administrative proposals reflects in an unusually public way the conflicts that normally surface privately within an administration's closed-door management conferences. These tensions may be ostensibly about achieving budget savings, but the differences often arise out of policy disagreements.

Conflicts among Fellow Travelers

Conflict need not be between institutional or political rivals. Fiscal tension can overcome partisan affinities, as the Democrats experienced in mid-1999. After the 1998 general election, Democrats held every statewide office and 60 percent of the seats in the Senate and the Assembly. Democrat Gray Davis won the gubernatorial election over his Republican challenger by a huge margin. Despite the apparent political hegemony for the Democratic Party, a bitter and public conflict erupted, evidencing a split between the governor and the Democrats' legislative leadership about how policy should be set. On July 11, 1999, the Davis administration called a meeting of a half-dozen legislative committee chairs to discuss the disposition of legislation before the health committees. The administration, the governor informed legislators, intended to direct the fate of specific fiscal bills without consulting either the authors or legislative leadership. The administration wanted to set both health policy *and* fiscal policy on these measures. Two days after the meeting,[2] the Democratic leadership, Assembly Speaker Antonio Villaraigosa and Senate pro Tempore John Burton, wrote a memorandum to the committee chairs, advising them to disregard their discussions with the governor. To protect the independence and integrity of the legislative branch, they told the members:

---

[2] Robert B. Gunnison and Greg Lucas, "Top Democrats Accuse Davis of Usurping Their Authority," *San Francisco Chronicle*, July 15, 1999, A-1.

We are not going to allow the legislative process to be dictated by executive department heads or administration staff. You are to pay absolutely no attention to any requests [from the administration] . . . .

These are strong words when criticizing a governor of your own party. To emphasize the locus of his differences with the governor, Senator Burton later said that the administration was making a "totally improper intrusion in the legislative process." The following week, Governor Davis acknowledged Burton's concern, but dismissed it as immaterial in light of his own electoral success,[3] saying

[The Legislature] has a totally different view of the world than I do, totally different. It was my vision that commanded a 20-point victory, the largest victory in 40 years. . . . People expect government to reflect the vision I suggested. Nobody else in the Legislature ran statewide. [The Legislature's] job is to implement my vision. That is their job.

It seems that process, especially when used to direct political outcomes, can ignite strong words and vastly different views about the appropriate role of the executive and legislative branches in setting fiscal priorities and policies governing basic program choices.

As suggested by this example, relations and negotiations on budget policy are particularly sensitive. One reason for this may be that the budget bill is unique among legislative measures considered by the Legislature. Presumably to prevent pork-barrel logrolling, the state constitution limits most bills to making a single appropriation.[4] Because only the budget bill may make appropriations to more than one program and from several funds it is the locus of fiscal attention.[5] While the Legislature could construct a budget using many bills each making single appropriations, it is impractical—if not physically overwhelming—to do so given the complexity of the state's finances. The budget bill, then, becomes the opportunity for the governor and Legislature to construct a single statutory statement yielding a comprehensive and balanced spending plan. To do so requires deft negotiation. Over time, the relative influence over the budget exerted by the executive and legislative branches has shifted back and forth and back again, depending on circumstances and the political acumen of the leadership.

Though the constitution divides fiscal responsibility between the legislative and executive branches, the executive and legislative branches need a way to man-

---

[3] Robert B. Gunnison, "Davis Says He Calls All the Shots," *San Francisco Chronicle*, July 21, 1999, A-1.

[4] Paragraph (d) of Section 12.

[5] In practice, language can be crafted to circumvent the prohibition on multiple appropriations in other bills, provided the appropriation is from one fund source (i.e., the General Fund). By making a single appropriation to the director of finance and then having control language direct a portion of the appropriation to other state entities, it is possible to make many appropriations within a bill.

age their differences and to minimize—or at least set boundaries on—conflict. No matter how difficult the negotiations become, legislators must understand the statutory requirements of the administration and the costs of financing those duties, if they are to budget successfully. For their part, governors are responsible for ensuring that the administration meets the intent of the legislative appropriations and the statutory responsibilities. Despite sometimes bitter language, the governor and the Legislature must collaborate on the budget. As such, the legislative budget process can be seen as a way of structuring the long negotiation to minimize conflict and to direct legislative efforts to passing a budget before adjournment.

The constitution specifically prohibits the executive from making appropriations without a two-thirds vote of each house (*c.f.,* Sections 1 of Articles III and IV of the state constitution). The Legislature cannot delegate to the governor its responsibilities for governing the state's finances. By identifying broad—and interdependent—roles for the governor and the Legislature, the constitution establishes a balanced and joint governance over state finances.

Not a Static Process

There is a tendency to overgeneralize about the legislative budget process, as if it were merely a set of unvarying steps that, if followed faithfully, produces the same results year-in and year-out, like preparing a recipe for apple pie. In practice however, there is no "cookbook" process for putting together the budget. Each year, the budget process changes as it responds to intrinsic dynamics, including personalities and fiscal conditions, and extrinsic dynamics such as national political trends. Though the law circumscribes the way the budget is crafted, the process adapts to these dynamics. Two recent examples illustrate the point:

- **Allies in negotiation can change**. In 2000, Democrat Robert Hertzberg had just become Speaker of the Assembly. His first objective in his new role was to assert a greater command over the shape of the budget. Typically, Assembly Republicans withhold their support for any budget compromise until the end of the budget process. Hertzberg believed if he could secure Republican votes for a budget in May—well before beginning negotiations with the governor or the Senate—he would change the budget dynamic to his favor. The Assembly, for a change, would be united in its negotiations. In mid-May, Hertzberg met with Scott Baugh, the Assembly Minority Leader at a private suite in the Los Angeles airport. They agreed to work on a common budget proposal that provided Republicans an early commitment from the Democratic leadership to a permanent $2 billion tax reduction.
- **Control over appropriations can shift**, though normally considered the province of the Legislature, between the branches. In December 2003, Governor Schwarzenegger's first director of finance, Donna Arduin, notified the Legislature that the administration would increase appropriations to immunize

local governments for losses sustained by a reduction in local revenues. Arduin contended that the $2.7 billion appropriation was consistent with statutory provisions delegating certain appropriations to the governor. The administration's actions appeared to the legislative analyst, however, to "represent major revision to legislative policy" and therefore an impermissible use of delegated power.[6] The Legislature had, in fact, adopted statutory language to prohibit the appropriation. Yet, Controller Steve Westly cut checks to the local governments for the higher reimbursement. (Later in the year, the Legislature adopted statutory language to do by statute what the governor had done by executive order.)

Despite its complexity and its changeable nature, the budget process is the means by which the state works out its spending plan. This chapter considers both the constitutional requirements and the informal budget steps taken to secure passage of the budget each year. After describing the legal requirements that divide responsibility between the executive and legislative branches, this chapter details the legislative calendar for completing the negotiations on the budget, and it discusses how the Legislature and governor collaborate to fashion a state budget.

Constitutional Provisions Divide Responsibility for the Budget

The Legislature and governor share responsibility for developing the state budget bill. Section 12 of Article IV, reproduced in Table 1.1, details the executive and legislative responsibilities.[7] The section's first five paragraphs succinctly delineate fiscal responsibilities without being proscriptive about either the content of or the process for writing—the budget.

The first paragraph in the section requires the governor to submit statements of recommended expenditures and estimated revenues. These statements are due to the Legislature by January 10. If recommended expenditures exceed the revenue estimate, then the constitution directs the governor to recommend sources for additional revenues. The constitutional language does not specify how detailed the "recommendations" must be, deferring instead to the governor's judgment. The governor's proposals are merely recommendations, as the section[8] reserves to the Legislature the submission, approval, and enforcement of budgets. In practice, governors provide a fully articulated proposal of expenditures and revenue for consideration by the Legislature. By January 10, Gover-

---

[6] Legislative Analyst's Office, *The 2004–05 Budget: Perspectives and Issues* (Sacramento, Calif.: Legislative Analyst's Office, February 2005), 136.

[7] Statutory law and administrative practice define additional responsibilities for the executive entities, while legislative traditions and rules circumscribe how the Legislature reviews and amends the bill. These provisions exercise much fewer constraints on the process, as they can be modified more readily by legislative action.

[8] Paragraph (e) of Section 12 of Article IV.

Table 1.1. Constitutional Responsibilities for Developing Budget Bill

Article IV of State Constitution

SEC. 12. (a) Within the first 10 days of each calendar year, the Governor shall submit to the Legislature, with an explanatory message, a budget for the ensuing fiscal year containing itemized statements for recommended state expenditures and estimated state revenues. If recommended expenditures exceed estimated revenues, the Governor shall recommend the sources from which the additional revenues should be provided.

(b) The Governor and the Governor-elect may require a state agency, officer, or employee to furnish whatever information is deemed necessary to prepare the budget.

(c) (1) The budget shall be accompanied by a budget bill itemizing recommended expenditures.

(2) The budget bill shall be introduced immediately in each house by the persons chairing the committees that consider the budget.

(3) The Legislature shall pass the budget bill by midnight on June 15 of each year.

(4) Until the budget bill has been enacted, the Legislature shall not send to the Governor for consideration any bill appropriating funds for expenditure during the fiscal year for which the budget bill is to be enacted, except emergency bills recommended by the Governor or appropriations for the salaries and expenses of the Legislature.

(d) No bill except the budget bill may contain more than one item of appropriation, and that for one certain, expressed purpose. Appropriations from the General Fund of the State, except appropriations for the public schools, are void unless passed in each house by rollcall vote entered in the journal, two-thirds of the membership concurring.

(e) The Legislature may control the submission, approval, and enforcement of budgets and the filing of claims for all state agencies.

---

nors Wilson, Davis and Schwarzenegger each submitted extensive *Budget Summaries* and *Budget Proposals*. Together, these two documents ran to hundreds of pages in each year. When their recommended expenditures exceeded estimated revenues, all three governors proposed not just "sources" of revenues but made specific revenue proposals.

The constitutional language does not require the governor to make proposals to balance the budget; it merely requires an identification of sources from which more revenue "should be provided." The letter of this language, if not its spirit, could be met with a gubernatorial statement vaguely referring to the sales or income tax.[9]

To meet its January 10 deadline—and to identify its priorities and challenges—the administration begins working in the prior April to collect the supporting information for the January submission. Representing the governor and managing the preparation of the budget is the Department of Finance. The department director serves on the governor's cabinet and is typically the most senior voice in the administration dealing with fiscal issues. Given these fiscal responsibilities, the director serves on many state boards.

In preparation for submitting the budget to the Legislature, the Department of Finance requires state agencies to develop baseline estimates for their costs associated with maintaining current programs, and to document justifications for budget expansions or reductions. The constitution[10] authorizes the governor to require any state agency, officer, or employee to furnish all information necessary to prepare the budget. When the governor submits the budget proposal in January, he or she places in bill format the recommended expenditures (that is, the governor must propose a budget bill with specific appropriations).[11] The bills must be introduced by the budget committee chair of each house.[12]

The constitution limits what the Legislature can do with the provisions of the budget bill. Though it may appropriate billions of dollars to a vast array of state programs, the budget may only make those appropriations consistent with current statute. The constitution specifically prohibits the budget bill from carrying any provision that would change the statutory provisions of law. In practice, however, when constructing the budget the governor and the Legislature often seek policy changes that require law changes. The changes may expand or contract programs, and they may raise taxes. The Legislature and governor may also seek changes to the state/local fiscal relationship as part of a negotiated budget. To authorize these changes, the Legislature adopts other bills, known colloquially as "trailer bills," contemporaneously with the budget bill itself.

Appropriations from the General Fund require a two-thirds vote of each house,[13] meaning that the budget bill must garner 27 votes in the Senate and 54 votes in the Assembly. Since 1992, no party has held a two-thirds majority in either house, so that any budget that passes requires a bipartisan compromise within each house. Effectively, the vote requirement means that one-third of either house can block a bill appropriating General Fund money. In recent years, budget votes have become more charged with partisan differences, with most or all the majority

---

[9] To the extent the state constitution requires a balanced budget, the reference is found in Article XVI. But even this article does not require the governor to propose a balanced budget.

[10] Paragraph (b), Section 12 of Article IV.

[11] Paragraph (c) (1) of Section 12 of Article IV.

[12] Paragraph (c) (2) of Section 12 of Article IV.

[13] Paragraph (d) of Section 12 of Article IV. Special fund appropriations can be made with a majority vote.

Democrats voting for the budget. Though all the Democrats have voted for the budget, they have not had the necessary two-thirds majority in either house. Since 1992, Republican votes in both houses have been necessary to secure passage. As a result, the budget nearly always reflects a negotiated settlement on the state's spending and tax policies among five parties: The governor, Assembly Democrats, Assembly Republicans, Senate Democrats, and Senate Republicans. The leader of the each caucus is typically the lead negotiator for the caucus's interests.

There is little statistical evidence that the two-thirds vote requirement changes gross spending or tax levels, and academic research provides decidedly mixed results. Of the five studies cited by Besley and Case, two established no statistical link between the supermajority requirements and fiscal outcomes. Two other studies showed that supermajority requirements could have a statistically significant impact on reducing taxes. Their own study indicated that tax and expenditure limitations had the "perverse" effect of leading to higher taxes.[14]

Though the statistical analysis cannot definitively identify changes in gross spending or tax levels, California's experience suggests that the budget reflects different outcomes because of the two-thirds requirement. For the period covered in this study, budget-related legislation generally passed with few spare votes. In the calculus of securing passage of the budget, the last vote has the same "demand value" whether it is the 21st vote in the Senate (as would be required with a majority-vote requirement) or the 27th vote (as is required under the two-thirds rule). But the last vote might be easier to secure under a majority-rule requirement, because the number of members who could "supply" the last vote is larger than under the two-thirds rule. Under a majority-vote condition, after 20 members have voted for the budget, the final vote could be cast by one of 20 other Senators. Under the two-thirds vote rule, when the budget has secured 26 votes, the final vote must be cast from one of the remaining 14 members. Under some circumstances, it would be easier to secure a vote from one senator of the 20 than it would be to secure the final vote from one of the 14.

The state's institutional rules and structures require a great deal of compromise and negotiation to secure passage of a budget. The executive and legislative branches share responsibility for constructing and approving the budget bill. Members of the two parties must cooperate to pass the budget bill. Should the governor or one of the legislative caucuses choose to, they can withhold their support of the budget and block the budget. As a result, the five parties to the budget must negotiate. Fiscal policy is shared between five parties.

---

[14] Timothy Besley and Anne Case, "Political Institutions and Policy Choices: Evidence from the United States," *Journal of Economic Literature*, vol. XLI (March 2003): 7–73.

New Constitutional Provisions Could Condition Future Negotiations

In 2004, Governor Schwarzenegger and the Legislature proposed to the state's voters three propositions that clarified and further limited the manner in which the state could construct the state's budget. The voters approved all three measures. Proposition 57 authorized the state to sell up to $15 billion in bonds to finance the state's accumulated General Fund debt. With this authority, the state borrowed from the private sector and pledged future tax revenues, for up to 15 years, for repaying the bonds.

Another measure, Proposition 58, attempted to place limitations on the way the way the state constructed its budget. It required that each budget contain a finding that the estimated revenues would cover estimated expenses for the year. Under the proposition, the state must set aside a growing share of revenues— eventually up to five percent of expenditures—for unanticipated expenses or lower-than-forecast reserves. The proposition also authorized the governor to take actions to bring the budget into balance in the event the state's fiscal condition deteriorated after the Legislature passed the budget.

Proposition 1A approved by voters in November 2004 generally prohibits the Legislature from using local revenues to balance the state's General Fund budget, though the Legislature has already discovered ways to circumvent its provisions.

Cumulatively, these measures can change the way the Legislature and governor negotiate, construct, and approve the budget. It is not clear how the Legislature or the governor will implement these provisions and whether the proposition will have an impact on fiscal prudence.

The Legislative Budget Calendar

The fiscal year starts on July 1 of each year, so it would be preferable if the budget were passed before the start of the fiscal year. If the budget passes on time, departments and the public will be certain that services will continue throughout the new fiscal year. The constitution requires the Legislature to pass the budget by June 15, but provides no sanctions if the deadline is missed.[15] The Legislature has not passed a budget before June 15 since 1984. In the 14 budgets passed since 1991, only four have been passed before the start of the fiscal year. So, budget delays are the norm.

Departments have learned to cope with the effects of budget delays. Many departments have had legislation enacted authorizing them to continue spending at the prior year's funded levels even if the budget is not signed. There are limits to how long departments can go without the budget, but it appears that all but a select few programs can maintain employment and services through September without a budget, the longest the state has ever delayed enacting a spending plan. It is not

---

[15] Paragraph (c) (3) of Section 12 of Article IV.

clear what would happen to employees or services if the budget were delayed until late fall.

The Legislature has adopted statutory language for some programs, referred to as a "continuous appropriation," that protects a program's funding even when there is no budget. A continuous appropriation is statutory language authorizing programs to spend money without having to receive an annual appropriation in the budget bill. One of the first continuous appropriations authorized by the Legislature made payments to bondholders. The continuous appropriation was intended both to insulate bondholders from the uncertainty of state budget negotiations and to ensure timely payments. When the state issues a bond to borrow money, the bondholders will lend at lower interest rates when they are more certain of being paid on time. The continuous appropriation provides that certainty. Since 1991, many income transfer programs have been granted continuous appropriation authority.

Public Hearings and Testimony from March until May.

As the constitution does not direct how the Legislature should organize itself for review and development of the budget (see Section 11 of Article IV), the budget process is a creature of legislative control and tradition. It begins each year after the governor makes the January budget proposal, and adapts to address changes in political and fiscal dynamics. In all, the Legislature takes at least six months—and as many as eight months—to review the governor's proposal, negotiate a compromise, and pass a budget. Though there is no set pattern, the Legislature must complete three specific tasks:

- Provide public forums for reviewing and evaluating budget alternatives.
- Accommodate revisions to revenue forecasts.
- Facilitate a five-way negotiation about the budget.

Legislative practice has been to accomplish these three tasks sequentially, so that they serve almost as phases for developing the legislative response to the governor's budget proposal. During the first phase, each house forwards the governor's budget proposal to each house's budget committee[16] for public review beginning in March. In this phase ending in mid-May, both the Assembly and the Senate devote hundreds of committee hours to public testimony about the consequences of the governor's proposal. During the second phase, beginning in mid-May, the governor and subcommittees re-evaluate the January budget proposal in light of changes in the economy and revenues. In the third phase, beginning in June, the Legislature and governor conduct a five-way negotiation on what the budget should include to secure sufficient votes to pass.

---

[16] In the Assembly, the committee is the Budget Committee. In the Senate, it is the Committee on Budget and Fiscal Review.

During the first phase, the budget committee plays a central role. The chair is responsible for managing the review of the proposal throughout the coming months. The quality and conduct of the legislative budget review, whether measured as the level of public access or the treatment of minority views, is a reflection of the chair's management and political skills. The legislative leadership—the Senate President pro Tempore, the Assembly Speaker, and the minority leadership—help to identify key budget issues during the first phase. During this initial public review period, the Legislature can modify the governor's budget and insert its priorities. For example, in 2001 Senator Steve Peace, chair of the Senate budget committee, challenged the governor in public. On January 10, 2001, Governor Davis proposed an $82.9 billion budget, four percent more than the previous budget. After the release of the budget, tax collections began to falter. By February, it appeared that the budget would have to be lower than proposed by the governor. So on March 2 Senator Peace convened a meeting of the full budget committee. Arguing that the state's economy was slowing and revenues would be lower than anticipated, he proposed that the full committee delete funding for all of the governor's new initiatives, saving about $2 billion. In the event the governor's revenue estimates proved accurate, Peace was confident that the Senate could find different ways to spend the $2 billion than the governor had proposed. The budget committee agreed to the cuts.

When the subcommittees began their deliberations, some subcommittees immediately restored the cuts made by the full committee. To keep the budget balanced, the subcommittees had to cut from other, base programs to finance the augmentations. More often, however, when the subcommittees augmented the governor's budget proposals, they did as Peace had predicted: They added to the budget to reflect their own, rather than the governor's, priorities.

The 2001 budget may have been unique. In most years, the legislative budget committees[17] start with the assumption of adopting the governor's budget as proposed in January. Making this assumption means that, if a subcommittee wants to deviate from the governor's January proposal, it must propose an amendment to what the governor has proposed.

The budget chairs are often assisted by the chairs of the Legislature's two other fiscal committees. The Revenue and Taxation Committee is responsible for hearing all legislation affecting General Fund taxes. In the budget context, the committee may analyze the impact of the revenue alternatives proposed by the governor and others. The Appropriations Committee is responsible for hearing all the legislation that has a fiscal impact but is not otherwise heard by the budget committee. If the state is running deficits, the committee may be asked to limit the

---

[17] For those interested in advocating before the subcommittees, two guides may be of interest, see: Rachel Lodge, Rebecca Gonzales, and Jean Ross, *Dollars and Democracy: An Advocate's Guide* (Sacramento, Calif.: California Budget Project, 2003), and California Senate Rules Committee, *The Budget Process: A Citizen's Guide to Participation* (Sacramento, Calif.: Senate Publications, November 2003).

cost of legislation it passes out of its committee. If the fiscal condition is healthy, the committee may be given a target for the cost of legislation it may pass.

The legislative analyst, the Legislature's nonpartisan budget expert, assists the Legislature's review during this period by preparing two major documents providing commentary and analysis about the budget. *The Analysis of the Governor's Budget* describes the governor's spending plan, typically by department or agency. Often, the analyst will recommend the Legislature reject or modify specific aspects of the governor's plan. Another document released by the analyst at the same, the *Perspectives and Issues,* provides a broader context for considering the budget by discussing the underlying economic, revenue, and expenditure trends, and other major fiscal issues. In mid-February, the analyst publishes two documents reviewing major aspects of the governor's proposal and providing context for the state's fiscal condition.

Sometime in March, the Assembly and Senate budget committees begin their separate public reviews of the budget. To manage the vast amount of detail associated with the budget items, each budget committee divides the work among five subcommittees. The subcommittees have jurisdiction over a broad range of related program areas. For example in 2009, the Assembly had five subcommittees, with a subcommittee responsible for education, natural resources, health and human services, information technology, and general government. The chair of the budget committee appoints the chair of each subcommittee and assigns legislative staff to support the work of the subcommittee.

There are usually three or five members on each subcommittee, with the Democrats holding the majority. They hold public hearings to review the governor's budget and consider the impact of the proposal. They may conduct oversight on issues of fiscal impact and importance. Typically, the subcommittees hold at least one hearing per week between the beginning of March and the middle of May. Every budget item assigned to the subcommittee may be heard before the end of May at least once, but a hearing is not necessary.

Through these hearings, the subcommittees review and publicize the budget. The written analyses prepared for the committee and the testimony at the hearings may improve legislators' understanding of what the governor has proposed, the implications of the proposals, and the alternatives. The hearings may also extend to the public an opportunity to address concerns. Before each hearing, the subcommittee staff members write an analysis, referred to as an "agenda," often describing the major proposals contained in the governor's budget. In the agenda, the budget committee consultant may include an analysis of the budget and provide context for the proposal. The consultant may include issues raised by the analyst in the *The Analysis of the Governor's Budget,* or by members of the Legislature and their staff. Typically, analyses are available at the hearing and may be available on each committee's website after the hearing.

Table 1.2 reproduces a typical issue raised in a committee analysis. The governor proposed a new program to allocate grants for subsidizing telecommu-

Table 1.2. Sample Issues from Budget Subcommittee Agenda

. . . [The governor] requests an appropriation from the High Cost Fund-A for $243,000 for three staff and $10 million in grants.

The commission staff have not provided any justification for the three staff beyond general descriptions of the workload. No justification has been provided for the specific work and staffing proposal. More significantly, there is no basis for estimating the need for the $10 million appropriation. The commission's application criteria and process will not be finalized for at least six months. Based on the available information, there is no way to predict the types of projects that will be funded or estimate whether the $10 million will be fully subscribed in the budget year.

Because the grants will not be awarded until the summer of 2003, it appears that this appropriation can be deferred until the 2003–04 budget without significantly affecting programs, if at all. By next year at this time, the commission will have a greater understanding of the likely pool of applicants and the cost of the grant awards.

. . . It is premature to make the appropriation until the commission . . . explains the criteria it will adopt and details the likely awards. . . . Consequently, staff recommend that the subcommittee . . . deny the appropriation.

Source: Senate Budget and Fiscal Review, *Compendium of Subcommittee Analyses 2002–03*. Sacramento, Calif.: State Publications. January 2003, 2–120.

---

nications services in low-income rural areas. The Governor requested $10 million for the grants, to be administered by the state's Public Utilities Commission. However, because this program was entirely new, the commission had no experience with the types of grant applications it would receive. It had no intelligence to assess the need for the program or the likely number of applicants. Under questioning by Senator Byron Sher, the chair of the Senate budget subcommittee, the commission admitted that it had not determined how it would evaluate the applications. Indeed, it did not know if it would complete the application review and award grants in the budget year. This proposal, then, had several problems. First, the Legislature had no context for determining if the $10 million request was too high, too low, or just right. The administration had not identified the budget need. Second, the commission had not identified the type of projects it would fund, so the Legislature had no chance to evaluate whether the $10 million would be spent on the Legislature's highest priorities. Third, the timing was wrong. Senator Sher recommended deleting the request on the grounds that the $10 million would not be spent in the budget year. He suggested that in another year, when the utilities commission had more fully assessed the problem and likely applications, the Legislature would be in a better position to evaluate the appropriateness of a $10 million program.

House rules prevent the subcommittees from amending the portion of the budget bill assigned to them. Instead, each subcommittee prepares a list of recommendations for action by the full committee. The subcommittees' recommendations are relative to the governor's January budget. The subcommittees present their recommendations to the full budget committee when they complete their work. Because the subcommittees cannot make amendments, there is no opportunity to display the effect of the subcommittee votes.

At the hearing, a representative of the legislative analyst may be asked to discuss the governor's budget and alternatives. The administration is represented by the Department of Finance and the department whose budget is being considered. The public may be invited to provide testimony.

Though the subcommittees cannot amend the bill, they take public votes on the recommendations. The recommendations are placed before the subcommittee as motions and may pass on a majority vote. The subcommittees can operate on a partisan basis, with the subcommittee actions reflecting the majority Democrats' position.

During the subcommittee process, each house and caucus generally pursues its own budget strategy. Though individuals—members or staff—may discuss widely their budget concerns and goals, the subcommittee process does not sustain a negotiation between the legislative caucuses. In part, this is because each caucus uses the subcommittee process to explore the impact of the governor's budget and its alternatives.

Nor does the subcommittee foster negotiations between the legislative caucuses and the executive branch. The administration's staff is not free to negotiate on the budget between January and May, as the governor revises the January proposal in May. Until this revision, the administration's staff would risk negotiating a change that did not represent the governor's later revision. Moreover, it is premature for the administration's staff to begin negotiating prior to the Legislature making a specific counter-proposal—approved by each house—to the January proposal.

So, the subcommittee process serves an "exploratory" function. As such, it tends to be partisan, and certainly positional. During the subcommittee process, the majority party constructs a budget that is essentially balanced, but which is merely a step in the negotiations. It is best seen as a "counter offer" to the governor's January proposal, but not necessarily a final offer in the negotiations.

When the subcommittee approves recommendations for amendments, there is no opportunity to display the changes to the public in March or April. The amendments are not available to the public until late May or early June, after the subcommittees have completed their work.

Each budget subcommittee tries to complete its work on the January proposal in early May, as they anticipate the governor's revision of the January proposals, which is scheduled for May 14.

Revised Revenue Estimates Precipitate a Major Change in the Governor's Budget Proposal.

Statutory law requires the governor to update the budget revenue forecast in May, and is known as the May Revision.

When the governor proposes a budget in January, he or she must make assumptions about how much revenue the state will collect over the next 18 months. To help quantify these assumptions, the Department of Finance uses a sophisticated revenue-forecasting model that relies on data about recent tax collections, and economic data about the state and national economy. The revenue forecasts cannot be made with precision, however. Economic models, like election surveys, have estimating error in the range of three percent to five percent. So, even when the models perform well, they can be off by as much as $4 billion for California's General Fund.

The estimates are updated as new tax and economic data become available. The corporations tax, which accounts for about 10 percent of General Fund revenue, is due on March 15. The income tax, due on April 15, accounts for about half of General Fund revenue. After these two taxes are paid and the returns processed, the Department of Finance re-estimates revenues for the next tax year based on collections for the current year. The governor releases the newer estimates on or before May 14, as required by statute. Since 1991, the new estimates have raised or lowered total revenue expectations by as much as 7.5 percent, increasing or reducing the amount of money available to balance the budget.

The recent experience with changed estimates are displayed in Table 1.3. The Department of Finance reduced its estimate of income tax revenues by $2.8 billion (4.8 percent) between December 2007 and May 2008. In the previous year, it raised its estimate of those tax revenues by $1.4 billion (2.7 percent).[18]

At the same time that the governor revises the revenue estimates, he or she will adjust the January spending proposal to account for changes in available revenues. If revenues are forecast to be lower, then the governor may propose reductions in total spending. If more revenue is estimated, the proposal may be to increase spending or cut taxes. In recent years, these new budget proposals, known collectively as the "May Revision," have contained significant changes to the January proposal.

---

[18] Department of Finance, *May Revision Summary,* 2007 and 2008.

Table 1.3. Change in Revenue Estimates January Governor's Budget and May Revision, 2006–07 through 2008–09 (Dollars in Millions)

	2006–07	2007–08	2008–09
Personal Income Tax	$201	-$362	-$2,725
Sales Tax	12	-506	-1854
Corporation Tax	406	237	-898
Insurance Tax	-54	-173	-247
Alcoholic Beverages Tax	0	0	0
Cigarette	-2	-2	-5
Other Revenue	-3	671	33

The subcommittees consider these proposals during the last two weeks of May. The budget subcommittees can complete their work as early as May 18 (as the Senate did in 2002), but typically work until the end of the month. There is little time for consideration or public review.

Most often, the administration uses the revision in May to update and change the Governor's Budget proposal. Sometimes the changes are major. For example, on May 14, 2000, with the state treasury awash in cash after unexpectedly high income tax payments on April 15, Governor Davis made a surprising announcement. After reviewing the state's fiscal condition, he proposed a major change in the state's income tax system, proposing that some teachers be excused from paying any income tax. The governor proposed the change as part of his revision to the January budget. For the governor, it was a way to increase teachers' post-tax income without having to increase the schools' budget. This change was significant because it was a departure from historical state tax policy. In the history of California's income tax, no class of taxpayer had been excluded from liability because of their profession.

It was a bold proposal from Governor Davis. Even more brashly, he had not mentioned this change before May 14, and though it was a major policy change, neither of the Legislature's tax committees had considered it. Nonetheless, Davis expected it to be adopted by the Legislature as part of the budget package due on June 15. Davis was using the May Revision, as Wilson had before him and as Schwarzenegger would after him, to surprise the Legislature.

While the revision is an opportunity for the governor to change the January budget proposal, it can be used to present major fiscal changes that might otherwise receive withering scrutiny during the subcommittees' review in March and April.

The May Revision is a signal to the subcommittees to complete their work and move the budget negotiations to a five-way discussion. Given the budget calendar, the Legislature has little time to review the May Revision. If the Legislature hopes to complete its review by the constitutional deadline of June 15, its subcommittees must complete their review of the governor's revised budget proposal, and allow time to complete the necessary five-way negotiation.

Around May 31, the subcommittees report their work to the full budget committee for amendment. In practice, the full committee rarely rejects the subcommittee's recommendations. Sometimes, the full committee will make changes to balance the budget if the sum of the subcommittees' actions would unbalance the budget.

After the full committee approves the subcommittee recommendations, the budget bill is amended, and referred to the full house for consideration. Each house may vote on the product of the subcommittees' work in the form of an amended budget bill. For many years, the Assembly Republicans considered the floor vote an opportunity to raise concerns about the budget prepared by the Assembly subcommittees, reflecting their disagreements with the subcommittee process and the decisions of the majority. In contrast, through most of the 1990s, the Senate Republicans viewed the vote on the subcommittee product to be a procedural step necessary to move the budget along to its next stage, the conference committee. In other years, both houses enjoy a full debate as the subcommittees' work product is considered.

In any event, after the majority in the Legislature has identified and crafted its counter-proposal to the governor's January budget, the negotiations for a final product can begin.

Five-Way Negotiations May Accelerate in June.

The versions of the budget adopted by the two houses will differ in significant ways from each other and from the governor's proposal, as each version reflects different priorities and interests expressed by the majority in each house. To resolve the differences, the Legislature convenes a conference committee consisting of three members from each house. Typically, each house appoints two members from the majority party and one member from the minority party. In this phase at the conference committee, the governor's representative is at the committee to speak for the governor as the committee develops an acceptable compromise. At the conference committee, the legislative parties and governor can begin to work toward a compromise acceptable to the Democrats, Republicans, and governor.

The Legislature's rules govern the conduct of conference committees. They may consider only those provisions of a bill that were approved by one or the other house. This rule is intended to prevent the conference committee from developing a compromise that has not been considered and approved by at least one of the houses. In recent practice, however, the conference committees ignore this rule.

While the conference committee represents a public forum, there may be a parallel private forum, known as the "Big Five." The "Big Five" includes the governor and four legislative leaders. Meetings are often held in the governor's office in the Capitol. To the extent that the leaders agree to a compromise, the conference committee is expected to adopt a budget to reflect the privately negotiated deal.

Once the conference committee adopts a compromise, it amends a bill, known as the conference committee report. The report is sent to each house simultaneously. The houses may not amend the report. If either house rejects the report, a new conference committee with different membership must be appointed. In addition to the budget bill, the conference committee refers to each house a set of bills which make statutory changes to implement a budget compromise.

Once the Legislature passes the budget package, the governor may reduce or eliminate most individual appropriations without having to veto the entire bill.[19] (The governor cannot, however, use a veto in the budget bill to eliminate an underlying continuous appropriation.) The practice of reducing appropriations is colloquially known as "blue penciling," as governors once used copy-editing pencils to mark appropriations for reduction. Governors have used their item-veto authority to reduce not only appropriations but to eliminate or change budget-control language. (The Legislature adopts control language to direct spending or limit the governor's discretion in the use of certain appropriations.) The Legislature, by a two-thirds vote in each house, can restore funding (and presumably, language) with a subsequent vote (known as a "veto override"), but it has not done so since 1979.[20] Consequently, the governor typically has the last word on appropriation levels contained in the budget bill. Table 1.4[21] displays the number and value of vetoes from 1991 through 2008, documenting the year-to-year variation in the number and value of vetoes.

The Executive and Legislative Branches Collaborate to Manage Fiscal Policy

Despite the complexity of the state's fiscal structure, each year the governor and Legislature negotiate a compromise on state spending. That they do so in an increasingly partisan era is remarkable. To many observers, balancing the state's budget must seem to be an elementary mathematical equation, requiring no greater skills than addition and subtraction. After all, how hard can it be to en-

---

[19] Paragraph (e) of Section 10.

[20] Rebecca LaVally, *Money and Power: A Look at Proposed Budgeting Changes in the Taxpayer Protection Act of 1992* (Sacramento, Calif.: Senate Publications, March 1992), 18.

[21] <http://www.dof.ca.gov/budgeting/budget_faqs/information/>.

Table 1.4. Number and Value of Governor's Vetoes General Fund and All Funds, 1991–92 through 2008–09 (Dollars in Millions)

	General Fund		All Funds	
	Number	**Amount**	**Number**	**Amount**
1991–92	40	$76.7	84	$193.5
1992–93	49	732.6	107	982.4
1993–94	28	3.8	85	32.2
1994–95	30	33.2	78	77.0
1995–96	8	2.1	65	166.5
1996–97	32	80.4	64	87.9
1997–98	43	298.4	103	336.8
1998–99	113	1,360,0	182	1,942.7
1999–00	106	521.3	149	833.2
2000–01	119	1,008.7	181	1,794.2
2001–02	109	498.9	170	658.3
2002–03	41	219.4	88	247.9
2003–04	11	1.0	19	47.2
2004–05	21	80.1	40	115.6
2005–06	40	114.5	93	319.7
2006–07	40	62.5	91	175.5
2007–08	51	702.8	108	1,399.7
2008–09	58	509.8	91	726.6

Source: Department of Finance, October 2008, Chart P-1.

sure that the state's income (predominately tax revenues) equals or exceeds spending? Yet, because negotiations are delayed until June 1, one month before the new budget year, the Legislature consistently misses the constitutional deadline. More often than not, the budget does not pass before the start of the fiscal year.

In most years, the Legislature passed the budget after the start of the fiscal year on July 1. Figure 1.1 shows when the budget passed in each year since 1991. Each year's budget is identified on the horizontal axis. On the right vertical axis, the graph identifies the date on which the budget passed its final house for each year. The left vertical axis measures the size of the General Fund budget. As displayed in the figure, the Legislature has not passed a budget by the constitutional deadline in any year between 1991 and 2006. During most of this period, the budget passed after the start of the new year. Of the 16 budgets displayed, only four budgets passed before the start of the new fiscal year.

Figure 1.1. Comparison of General Fund Expenditures and Date Budget Bill Chaptered, 1991–92 through 2008–09 (Dollars in Millions)

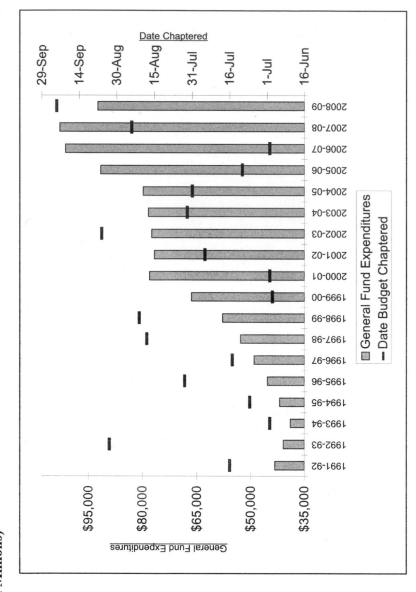

The figure demonstrates that the amount of delay is not a function of either the size of the budget or its rate of growth. These budget delays are often seen as a symptom of the Legislature's insufficient discipline in managing its own work calendar and the state's fiscal affairs. This chapter suggests an alternative: Delay is primarily a function of the budget calendar and the difficulty in negotiating a five-way agreement.

Successful budgeting requires a high degree of collaboration and cooperation, with three characteristics to describe the current process:

1. The Governor Controls Information.

By proposing a comprehensive budget in January, the governor frames the budget debate: What is the budget problem? What are viable solutions? The budget proposal signals what kind of tax increases and program changes the governor will entertain. The governor's January budget proposal colors the debate that follows.

The governor's command over the Department of Finance and other departments can also limit the kind of information released to the Legislature and the public throughout the budget process. The May Revision, too, affords the governor the opportunity to simultaneously incorporate any new ideas promulgated by the Legislature and to reassert the administration's original interests.

2. Process Is Important, But Is Not a Substitute for Content.

Managing the process is important. When Governor Schwarzenegger declared his first budget finished just before the July Fourth holiday, he seemed to have accomplished his goal of delivering a budget around the start of the fiscal year. But there were some loose ends—primarily dealing with the tricky negotiations around local finance reform—that were not completed. He did not meet with the legislative leadership over the Independence Day holiday. When they did meet later in the week, the "deal" the governor had declared so triumphantly the week before had vanished. So, budget negotiations had to be restarted, and they dragged on through the summer days in Sacramento.

While the process cannot dictate solutions, it can, when managed well, facilitate productive and expeditious negotiations.

3. Though the Process Is Porous, Public Access Is Limited.

Given the number of hearings and the length of time it takes to negotiate a budget, there are many opportunities to influence the process. However, the opportunity for public testimony and formal input is limited to the subcommittee hearings held between March and early May. The public has no opportunity to testify after release of the May Revision or during conference committee deliberations.

Departments rarely[22] have inherent authority to spend revenues deposited in the state treasury. Rather, the state constitution grants to the Legislature the exclusive power to authorize state spending. To exercise this power, the Assembly and Senate must act—typically, the Legislature must pass a bill—typically with a two-thirds majority through each house. If a state entity cannot spend revenue without legislative action, then the Legislature can use its authority to reduce, redirect, or expand a department's activities by changing its funding. The constructive use of the Legislature's discretion to appropriate enhances its ability to set expenditure policy, to direct management practices, and to establish broader public policy.

Most spending is authorized in the annual Budget Act, though an appropriation may be made in other legislation. Outside the budget process, the Legislature considers a broad range of issues with fiscal consequences. When considering law changes, the Legislature assesses program objectives and priorities. It can direct administrative practices when passing law changes. It uses changes in statutory law to establish departmental governance and discretion of administrative autonomy. The state directives affect departmental costs. These directives and changes can impose administrative and programmatic costs on departments.

General Fund appropriations, generally, must be approved by two-thirds of the membership of each house. This supermajority requirement can create a *practical* imperative for bipartisan negotiations on expenditure policy. Because Democrats have held a majority, but rarely a two-thirds majority, bills making General Fund appropriations have relied on votes from Democratic and Republican members in both the Assembly and the Senate. When the state has had a Republican governor, Republican legislators have tended to withhold their votes until the governor agreed to the legislation. In this way, the supermajority on budgets forces the Democratic majority to coordinate with Republican governors.

The governor has a limited number of days to approve or veto legislation. Failing to act within the prescribed days would allow legislation, including appropriations, to become law without gubernatorial approval.

The governor may veto this legislation or may reduce an appropriation in any legislation. By granting the governor veto authority, the constitution circumscribes the Legislature. Because the governor has this authority, the Legislature cannot act unilaterally, but must consider gubernatorial reactions to legislation. As a result, the legislative and executive branches tend to collaborate. However, because the

---

[22] One of the rare exceptions to this shared responsibility was granted by the voters in a statewide initiative. When they approved Proposition 162 (1992), the voters authorized the state's public pension systems to draw directly on state funds to pay for pension-system administration and to make payments on retirement benefits.

Legislature must first authorize spending, the governor generally cannot initiate spending.

The state constitution also grants the governor the authority to reduce or eliminate any single line of appropriation. This power, referred to as the "line item veto," can be used on any appropriation, whether in the budget bill or in other legislation. While the Legislature can override a veto with a two-thirds vote of each house, the Legislature has not seriously considered overriding a governor's veto in the last 15 years. With an effective threat of a veto, the governor has significant discretion to reject or reduce legislation making appropriation. This discretion often gives the executive disproportionate influence over the size and nature of an appropriation made by the Legislature.

The governor also influences the use of an appropriation by directing the way programs are administered. Article V of the state constitution makes the governor responsible for implementing statutory law and grants the governor administrative discretion to assign functions within state administration. The governor has control over employment and personnel practices. Using its administrative prerogatives, the executive branch exerts enormous control over the efficiency and product of the state bureaucracy. In 2007,[23] the executive had authority to hire and manage 202,224 staff directly in state government and another 131,675 personnel in higher education. No amount of specific law can effectively limit these management prerogatives.

In much the same way as with appropriations, the Legislature and governor collaborate to raise or lower taxes. The Legislature must initiate tax reductions, and can lower taxes with a majority vote of each house and the signature of the executive. It must also initiate legislation raising taxes with a two-thirds vote of both houses and a governor's signature. The Legislature could unilaterally raise taxes by overriding a governor's veto with a two-thirds vote of each house, but overrides on tax measures are unprecedented in California. In practice, the two-thirds vote requirement and the state's political climate have limited the number of tax increases approved by the Legislature since 1991.

The Legislature's power to establish fiscal policy is tempered by the governor's authority to approve or veto the legislation authorizing spending. Each year, the governor and the Legislature successfully resolve differences on a myriad of fiscal issues. In practice, the balance of authority can shift between the executive and legislative branches. Because the power to appropriate is central to each branch's ability to make and sustain policy, the outcome of the fiscal negotiations is of particular interest and sensitivity to each party.

---

[23] Department of Finance, *Governor's Budget*, 2009, Schedule 4.

Illusory Fiscal Consensus

Budgets are not the measure of great societies. By themselves they cannot comfort the sick or shelter the poor. They do not build world-class universities or pave roads. Budgets are not an end in themselves, but they serve as a kind of financial plan that identifies the state's policies, preferred services, and priorities. For example, when in 2008 Governor Schwarzenegger proposed closing state parks in order to help finance expansions in prisons and Medi-Cal, Californians could see his policy and service priorities.

When constructing the state's budget, political leaders face a numbing array of choices. If the consequences were merely a matter of indifference, like the result of choosing among restaurant entrees, then the annual budget delay would be neither difficult nor interesting. But recent budgets, particularly in cumulative effect, have daily impacts to most Californians, from opening hours at the branch library to commute conditions on roads, from the size of elementary school classes to the extent of prison health care.

Perhaps these challenges could be muted if the number of policy choices were more limited. To the grandparents of today's retirees, the state provided little health care or assistance. In 2007, the state treasurer wondered aloud whether the state could continue to finance university-level education in the state. But spending choices are not easily limited. Few Californians would countenance reducing Medi-Cal subsidies or privatizing the University of California system. For the immediate future, it seems, the policy choices inherent in the budget will remain deep and broad.

In practice, passing the budget is made more difficult by the way the state's institutions divide fiscal decisions among the governor, the Senate, and the Assembly. Because two-thirds of each legislative house and the governor must agree on the provisions of the budget bill, consensus is at a premium. As described in later chapters, the Legislature and governor negotiate and revise the budget through a formal process.

They also subscribe voluntarily to an informal set of norms. Their general adherence to these norms helps the principal parties work through an almost limitless number of issues by clarifying the bases for "acceptable" compromises. These norms include:

1. Defer to the Executive Branch to Define the Terms of the Budget

The executive branch collects and reports much of the information used in tracking budget expenditures and revenues. It is responsible for meeting statutory mandates, so each agency must track program demand and performance. Departments collect information on program expenditures and personnel for internal management purposes and for reporting much of the data to other state agencies.

They report, for example, expenditure information to the state controller's office and staffing information to the Department of Personnel Administration.

For purposes of developing the budget, the governor relies on the Department of Finance, which serves as the administration's budget expert and fiscal watchdog, to collect the budget information from agencies. In addition to collecting and compiling the information, it estimates demographic changes and forecasts revenues. The department is the governor's most important fiscal advocate.

For putting together the 2009–10 budget, the Department of Finance distributed instructions to agencies in May 2008, over a year before the start of the budget. Agencies logged thousands of hours collecting, recording, and presenting the data required to the department. They submitted thousands of pages of schedules and forms detailing the programmatic, fiscal, and personnel aspects of their budgets. The volume of information generated each year cannot possibly be reviewed, much less mastered, by any single person.

When presenting the budget, the Department of Finance compiles much of the information for dissemination to the Legislature and the public. The department prepares information on capital outlay, and on federal and local budgets. The information presented answers the essential questions about the governor's budget proposal. How much was spent last year? What are the caseload increases likely to be in the budget year? How much revenue from state and federal sources is likely to be available for spending in the budget?

The Legislature, too, uses the information developed and presented by the Department of Finance.[24] By using a common set of data, whose bases and continuities are generally accepted by all parties, the Legislature and governor minimize the disputes over the authority of the data they use to make decisions. In this way, the norm provides a common point of reference.

2. Pass a Complete, 12-Month Budget Package

The Legislature strives to adopt a budget before the start of the new fiscal year, specifying most of the state's annual appropriations in a single, comprehensive document. Any accompanying legislation—a "trailer bill"—is also adopted by the Legislature simultaneously with the budget bill.

If the California Legislature were to follow a less comprehensive approach, it could adopt piecemeal budgets as it negotiated compromises on areas of spending. It could, for example, create separate budgets for transportation, education, health, and resources programs. Instead, the Legislature combines all

[24]The Legislature's own budget experts in the Legislature Analyst's Office review and comment on this information. The legislative analyst's office describes itself as California's nonpartisan fiscal and policy analyst and provides the Legislature and the public invaluable independent analysis of the administration's information. It does not, however, have sufficient staff to counter the work of the administration.

negotiated aspects of the budget into a package for a single vote. By doing so, it mitigates the difficult votes for the members. Because all budgets contain objectionable aspects, a comprehensive package affords legislative members the chance to vote for an entire spending proposal that includes many acceptable aspects to balance out the objectionable parts.

The Legislature also strives to have a 12-month budget package in order to avoid having to adopt temporary, or stop-gap, budgets. By contrast, after missing the July 1 start of the fiscal year, legislators could authorize a one-month budget to give the governor and the Legislature more time to complete their negotiations on the overall budget. The Legislature did this for a month in 1992. Since then, however, the Legislature has worked to have a comprehensive, single budget. A comprehensive budget, then, provides sustained pressure to complete the Legislature's work while reducing the number of time-consuming and distracting exercises of adopting temporary budgets.

3. Concentrate on the General Fund

The Legislature focuses almost exclusively on the General Fund during the budget process. In part, this is because the General Fund accounts for over two-thirds of the funds appropriated, but it is primarily because the Legislature has the greatest amount of discretion over the allocation of General Fund revenue. It can reallocate savings from a General Fund appropriation to any other program area. So the Legislature can cut General Fund appropriations for the arts to be used for an increase in funding for parks. (Special fund revenue cannot be reallocated so broadly.) By concentrating its efforts on the use of the General Fund, the Legislature narrows the number of programs and issues it must negotiate.

4. Have Beneficiaries Pay

Because General Fund expenditures receive greater scrutiny, the Legislature places a premium on shifting the cost of programs to non-General Fund revenue sources. If it can find a way to charge a beneficiary, it can shift costs from the General Fund to the "user." For example, in the mid-1990s, it reduced General Fund support for state parks and increased the fees for day-use permits and parking.

When it shifts the funding of programs to beneficiaries, the Legislature tends to reduce its oversight of those programs. It tends to assume that user fees can often approximate a "market transaction" of willing "buyers" purchasing governmental services. By narrowing the breadth of programs and issues reviewed in the budget process, the shift to user fees reduces the challenges to completing a budget.

5. Rely on Making Incremental Changes

In most years, the Legislature funds a program at the same amount—after accounting for changes in costs and caseload—it appropriated in the prior budget. This helps provide continuity in service provision and reduces the amount of time the Legislature needs to review programs it has already approved. When continuing the spending and policies of the prior year's budget, the Legislature is said to be approving a "baseline" budget. The "baseline" will get adjusted for changes in caseload and costs, but generally will not get much legislative scrutiny. By concentrating on increases or decreases in program services, an "incrementalist" approach allows the Legislature to focus its budget work on those fewer budgets where it may want to make changes.

6. Be Selective about Making Programmatic Changes through the Budget

The budget document is a simple listing of appropriations—authority for departments to spend a specified amount over the 12-month period starting on July 1. It is a very poor document for dictating management decisions, such as determining who should be hired or the proper terms for a work product. Neither the budget document itself nor any trailer bill facilitates management changes. By focusing on the amount of the appropriation, the Legislature can defer many decisions to the policy committees or other subsequent legislative action.

Conclusion

California's experience with budget rules and norms is not unique. Congress and other states use informal and formal processes for organizing their review of budgets. Wildavsky discussed Congress's tendency to accept certain standards for budget construction and negotiation.[25] In a more recent review of the efficiency of congressional budget rules, Penner and Steurele[26] note that institutional rules are easy to disparage because they may appear arbitrary, and they do not produce results supported by all parties. Their utility derives not from achieving an "optimal" solution, but from providing a procedural structure for completing most budget negotiations.

California's norms operate largely out of custom and serve as voluntary limitations on the types of information and behavior considered appropriate when ne-

---

[25] Aaron Wildavsky, *The New Politics of the Budgetary Process* (2d ed.) (New York: HarperCollins, 1992), 416.

[26] Rudolph G. Penner and C. Eugene Steuerle, "Budget Rules," *National Tax Journal* LV II, no. 3 (September 2004): 547–52.

gotiating the state budget. They clarify how issues may be successfully negotiated and what must be resolved prior to passing the budget. By setting parameters to the negotiations, they help facilitate decision-making and minimize conflict.

All parties to the negotiation benefit from an articulated process and activities that encourage predictability, stability, and transparency in decisions and negotiations. Many of the formal and informal rules and norms are designed to channel amicable resolutions.

Developed over the years, these norms will continue to evolve as fiscal and political conditions change. Because they are voluntarily accepted by all parties in the negotiation, their application and utility vary as political conditions change. This means they can be disregarded or circumvented.

Beyond these formal procedures and informal norms, perhaps the budget bill itself most effectively narrows the issues subject to budget negotiations. As a piece of legislation strictly limited to making appropriations, it has a narrow scope. Through the bill, the Legislature and governor provide only broad direction about how the appropriated funds can be spent. The bill lists each entity receiving an appropriation and reflects spending for a single year. Though it serves as a spending plan covering a 12-month period, it is not a substitute for long-term planning. For the same reason, it cannot function as an adequate capital investment plan for the state.

This shorter timeframe can affect the way decisions are made. The Legislature and the governor can use the 12-month scope of the budget to shift costs beyond the 12 months covered in the Budget Act. For example, the Legislature can "balance" this year's budget by using revenues from next year. It can adjust budget accounting to "recognize" this year's costs in next year's budget. In this way, the 12-month budget bill creates incentives to make short-term decisions whose out-year consequences are discounted.

Even as these limits help the Legislature to expedite its budget decisions, they are criticized for facilitating budget resolutions that produce expedient decisions rather than providing more substantial fiscal review. There is a tension, never fully resolved in the state's budget process, between completing the negotiations on a timely basis and making prudent budget decisions.

Chapter 2

Managing the State's Fiscal Condition

Staff milled around the governor's office with a certain expectation in the early hours of June 17, 1993. They had heard rumors of an imminent budget compromise. After enduring 1992's record-setting budget delay, everyone seemed relieved with the prospect of a resolution before the start of the fiscal year. During the day, the pace of negotiations had certainly taken on an urgency. Since the late afternoon, the four legislative leaders and the governor had sequestered themselves in the Ronald Reagan Conference Room, a large space just outside the governor's private office in the Capitol. Suddenly, sometime after 2:00 a.m., Assembly Speaker Willie Brown burst from the room and gathered the staff together. The governor and legislative leadership, he said, had agreed on all outstanding budget issues, but were $100 million short of balancing the budget. Did anyone have any ideas that could generate revenue or savings?

At first, the staff stared back in silence at the speaker. No, they had advanced all their ideas over the last six months. When their proposals were deemed prudent, they had already been incorporated into the compromise budget. After a few moments of uncomfortable silence, someone spoke from the back of the crowd. The speaker's own staff—together with budget staff from both houses—had been working for nearly a year with the Department of Motor Vehicles on a proposal to improve collection of the annual car tax. The department, it seemed, did not have the facility or the inclination to pursue payments from late taxpayers. If leadership agreed to transfer the responsibility for collecting the delinquencies to the Franchise Tax Board—which was quite practiced in increasing tax collections— revenues could be increased by $100 million in 1993–94 and about $50 million for each subsequent year.

Brown knew that the tax board had a strong record of collecting from dead-beats, but he eyed the assembled staff suspiciously. Was the estimate realistic? Would Governor Wilson and the Republican leaders agree to increased tax efforts? How would his caucus react to giving the tax board a "hunting license" on collecting taxes? After weighing the proposal, he broke a faint smile. Wheeling around, he cackled and returned to the conference room. Fifteen minutes later, the leadership concluded its negotiations, and "awarded" the tax board a new responsibility for collecting $100 million in delinquent car taxes in 1993–94.

It was easy making the statutory change to expand the Franchise Tax Board's responsibilities. The Legislature merely added a sentence to the state's tax code declaring the board responsible for collecting past-due vehicle taxes, starting in mid-1993.

As a practical matter, however, the Franchise Tax Board was not prepared to take on the responsibility of collecting from thousands of deadbeat car owners. While the board collected billions of dollars in delayed income and corporation taxes, it had no experience locating car owners or working the accounts of delinquent drivers. To make the change successful, the Department of Motor Vehicles would have to transfer to the tax board all its files on the thousands of individual car owners and their late accounts. The tax board would have to hire new collections staff—or transfer the existing department staff—to work the accounts. So, the budget bill was changed to add financing for the information exchange, reducing the motor vehicle department's staff and increasing the tax board's staff.

Then, the Legislature had to make sure that the new revenue accrued to the state's benefit. Because the state constitution earmarks the car tax revenue to local government, the increased taxes would be allocated directly to cities and counties, without any benefit to the state's General Fund. To have the changes benefit the state, legislative staff formulated a series of financial transactions to rinse the revenue gain of its local earmark and make sure the state General Fund gained the $100 million. Property tax revenue, which would have gone to the cities and counties, was shifted to the schools by an amount equal to the higher car-tax revenues. The higher property tax revenue allocated to schools would offset—dollar for dollar—the state's support of schools. In this way, the state benefited from an increase in *local* revenue collections. Staff dubbed this mechanism a "roundabout," naming the cumbersome series of transactions after a "traffic calming" road obstruction that requires cars to travel 270 degrees around a traffic circle when making a 90-degree left turn. Before parking the local revenue in the state's General Fund, the Vehicle License Fee "roundabout" mechanism required the new revenue to travel the long way around.

Taken in its broader context, the roundabout mechanism was more than a last-minute budget gimmick to generate more revenue out of the tax system. It was intended to improve tax fairness and compliance within the state and local tax system—after all, everyone should pay their legal share of taxes. Through the change, the state would expect to better identify, target, and collect from tax deadbeats, for 1993 and future years. To be successful in achieving permanent and stable change, the negotiators had to have a sophisticated understanding of both the state/local fiscal structure and the relationship among administrative entities within the state's revenue system. They understood that the state's fiscal structure was more than the compilation of expenditures in the Budget Act. Which revenue streams flow to state and local coffers? Under what circumstances can the state redirect local revenues? What are the relative strengths of the state's tax agencies? When responsibilities for state administration are shared, to what extent do independent bureaucracies work together? What incentives would encourage better "performance"?

The roundabout maneuver illustrates how even a simple change—like shifting administrative responsibility between departments—becomes complex when used to achieve fiscal and policy goals. Nor is the roundabout a unique example of increasing fiscal complexity. With every legislative session, the governor and Legislature add more complications in the state's fiscal structure. This increased complexity demands greater sophistication and insight when managing the state's finances.

Given the size of the budget and the consequences for mismanaging the state's fiscal affairs, Californians should expect that the fiscal structure is managed well. A well-managed structure would ensure that state revenues are employed to their highest and best use, that fiscal decisions are made on a prudent financial basis, and that spending properly prepares the state for sustained prosperity.

Whom should Californians hold accountable for managing the state's fiscal structure? The introductory chapter described why the executive and legislative branches collaborate to pass a budget. The state's fiscal policy structure—which entails much more than the annual budget—involves not only the Legislature and governor but the electorate in the management of state finances. While the electorate can exercise direct control in limited ways, the executive and the Legislature collaborate in the ongoing management of the state's fiscal structure. All play a role in directing state funds or establishing revenue streams. Each can change the size and nature of state appropriations. This chapter describes how the electorate, governor and Legislature combine to set fiscal policy. It considers how the current protocols and practices limit the Legislature's effectiveness in directing and implementing fiscal policy, and concludes with an assessment on the limitations of the budget document itself.

The Electorate Provides Incomplete and Episodic Management of the State's Fiscal Structure

The voters can make fiscal policy directly when they consider properly framed propositions in statewide elections. Propositions can be placed on the ballot by two means. One is by initiative, which places a proposition on a statewide ballot after a sufficient number of voters sign a petition. Proposition 13 (1978) is the state's most famous fiscal initiative. Its immediate effect was to halve local property taxes and limit their growth in subsequent years. The reduced revenue stream limited local governments' ability to expand programs. But it did much more to change the fiscal environment.

The Legislature, too, may place a question before the voters, if a majority in each house approves a resolution to place a measure on a statewide ballot. Though the governor does not have the opportunity to approve or veto a legislative proposition, governors often propose or negotiate issues placed by the Legislature before the voters.

Some ballot measures raise revenues or earmark funds. For example, Proposition 163 (1992) reduced the very taxes the Legislature had raised in 1991. (In 1991, the Legislature imposed taxes on snack foods, sodas, and bottled water.) Proposition 42 (2002) directed the proceeds of taxes imposed on motor fuels, like gasoline, to fund transportation projects. It limited the Legislature's ability to reallocate this revenue to nontransportation programs. Proposition 49 (2002) directed the Legislature to fund after-school programs. By creating earmarks, these propositions dedicated a revenue stream to transportation projects and programs. Proposition 1A (2006), a follow-up to Proposition 42, strengthened and clarified the rules for the use of taxes on motor fuels.

Though these propositions are intended to be "self financing," they may not enhance the state's "fiscal capacity." Propositions raising taxes may merely soak up the available tax capacity, limiting the state's ability to raise other taxes in the future.

Table 2.1 summarizes the fiscal propositions approved by the voters since 1978. These propositions can have small fiscal effects—Proposition 49 provides less than $500 million for after-school programs. Or they can have large effects—Proposition 63 raised and allocated billions of dollars more for mental health programs than would have ever been provided as part of the legislative budget. Irrespective of their effects on individual programs, however, statewide elections are a poor mechanism for addressing the state's fiscal condition comprehensively.

Whether any of these propositions actually simplify or improve decisions is often hotly debated between supporters and opponents. What is not debatable is that these initiatives affect the way fiscal decisions are made or implemented. For example, Proposition 162 (1992) prohibits the Legislature and governor from directing the actuarial findings of the public retirement funds, such as the California State Teachers Retirement System. This change grants the retirement system significant independence to manage the retirement system's assets and funding condition. After the electorate's approval of the proposition, the Legisla-ture would find it hard to construct a budget assuming a higher rate of investment earnings for purposes of calculating the state's annual retirement contribution, as it did in 1991.

Even if they do not direct the Legislature to take specific actions, propositions can change the way fiscal matters are discussed in Sacramento. For example, Proposition 98 (approved in 1988 and described as providing a funding minimum for schools) effectively divided the General Fund budget into two streams—one stream dedicated to K-14 schools and the other to the rest of the budget. By segre-

Table 2.1. Comparison of Approved Propositions by Type

	Election Year	Effect
Mainly Procedural		
Proposition 13	1978	Requires two-thirds vote of Legislature to increase taxes
Proposition 4	1979	Limits spending by state
Proposition 98	1988	Establishes minimum state funding for schools
Propositions 108 & 111	1990	Establishes a process for funding transportation and transit. Revises Proposition 98
Proposition 162	1992	Limits the Legislature's authority over actuarial practices at public retirement systems
Proposition 58	2004	Requires a balanced budget and restricts debt
Proposition 1A	2006	Requires that fuel tax revenue be directed to transportation
Mainly Revenue Earmarks		
Proposition 163	1992	Prohibits imposition of sales tax on food
Mainly Expenditure Earmark		
Proposition 49	2002	Requires state to finance after-school programs
Raise and Direct Revenue		
Proposition 99	1988	Imposes 25-cent per pack tax on cigarettes for health programs
Proposition 10	1998	Imposes 50-cent per pack tax on cigarettes to finance childhood programs
Proposition 42	2002	Directs taxes on motor fuel to transportation
Proposition 63	2004	Imposes surcharge on millionaires income to fund mental health programs
Proposition 1A	2004	Restricts state from redirecting local revenues

gating a portion of the General Fund to schools, the proposition can be seen to separate school funding choices as tradeoffs with other parts of the budget. Irrespective of whether the proposition changed the actual amount of funding allocated to schools, it changed the way the budget is discussed.

Propositions can have surprising results too. Proposition 13, written to limit local discretion in raising property taxes, had the unintended effect of requiring the Legislature to allocate property tax revenue. (Prior to adoption of Proposition 13, each local agency had authority to levy its own tax on property, thereby ensuring revenue independence from the state.) This shift of revenue control from local governments to the state changed the relationship between the state and local governments. After the implementation of Proposition 13, the state could direct the property tax revenues to meet its, rather than local, objectives. Between 1992 and 2004, the state shifted billions of dollars away from local governments, using the authority granted by Proposition 13. Proposition 1A, approved by the voters in 2004, limited the state's ability to reallocate revenues from local agencies.

Proposition 13 also increased the number of votes needed to raise taxes. This higher vote threshold has a large and continuing influence on fiscal decisions. When private entities have reviewed the state's financial condition and evaluated its creditworthiness, they have found very great weaknesses. In recent years, they have consistently ranked California below its peer states. In lowering the state's ranking, the credit rating agencies cite the cumulative effect of fiscal propositions that limit the discretion the governor and Legislature have for managing the state's finances

Table 2.2 excludes those propositions authorizing the issuance of debt, though the voters must approve the debt before it can be sold on the bond market. This debt, secured with General Fund revenues and known as general obligation debt, is usually reserved for projects with a longer life (such as land acquisition and school-building construction). One exception, approved by voters in 2004, is a $15 billion bond issue used to finance the state's rollover deficits in 2003-04. While the voters must authorize the issuance of any general obligation debt, if there are no appropriate projects, the treasurer will not issue the debt.

Because the bond-repayment costs are financed out of the General Fund, issued bonds commit the state's future taxpayers—for a period typically of 30 and 40 years—to service the debt. On July 1, 2006, the state had a total of $37.1 billion of outstanding General Obligation bonds. Of this amount, about $11.3 billion were associated with the rollover debt. It had a total of $26.6 billion authorized but unissued.[1] With the voters' approval of the bond package on the November 2006 ballot, debt costs will increase when the treasurer issues this new debt.

---

[1] Phillip Angelides, *The State of California 2006 Debt Affordability Report*, 3.

Table 2.2. PPIC Survey: Selected Responses to Questions about Initiative Process, August, September, October 2006

Responses of Likely Voters

Question	Response	Percent Responding
Do you think it is a good thing or a bad thing that a majority of voters can make laws and change public policies by passing initiatives?	Good Thing	74
	Bad Thing	21
	Don't Know	5
Do you think public policy decisions made through the initiative process by California voters are probably better or probably worse than public policy decisions made by the governor and state Legislature?	Better	60
	Worse	24
	Same	6
	Don't Know	10
Do you agree or disagree: There are too many propositions on the state ballot?	Agree	58
	Disagree	38
	Don't Know	4
Do you agree or disagree: The ballot working for citizens' initiatives is often too complicated and confusing for voters to understand what happens if the initiative passes?	Agree	79
	Disagree	19
	Don't Know	2

Propositions Remain Popular with Voters

With increasing frequency in recent elections, the state's voters have approved propositions directing or limiting the way the Legislature and governor can craft a budget or manage the state's finances. Since 1978, the voters have approved 13 propositions directed at the state's fiscal structure. Six of these propositions were approved between 2004 and 2008. Often, supporters of propositions justify their proposals as directing, simplifying, and improving the way financial decisions are made. Between 1978 and 2008, the voters approved six propositions to change the process or rules by which the Legislature or governor make fiscal decisions. Proposition 13 required the Legislature to approve tax increases with a two-thirds vote in each house. Proposition 4 (1979) imposed a limitation on the amount of appropriations. These two propositions mark the start of an era in which voters expressed suspicion about how the governor and Legislature make fiscal decisions. Proposition 98 (1988) established an annually adjusted funding minimum for state schools and limited the Legislature's discretion to reallocate funding away from K-14 schools. It is often cited as an example of "ballot-box budgeting" that attempted to limit legislative discretion. Proposition 162 (1992) limited the Legislature's authority over actuarial practices at public retirement systems. Proposition 58 (2004) required the Legislature to construct and adopt a balanced budget, and was intended to limit the Legislature's discretion to assume debt in financing programs in the budget year. Proposition 1A, approved in a later election in the same year, prevented the Legislature from redirecting local revenues.

The electorate remains supportive of using propositions to set fiscal policy, as the Public Policy Institute of California found in a survey prior to the November 2006 election. It asked likely voters about the state's propositions and the initiative process and found support for—along with a healthy dose of skepticism about— the use and effect of propositions. Most California voters want the chance to advance policy directly through propositions and make the changes with a simple majority vote of the statewide election. Nearly three out of four voters agreed that it was a "good thing" to make laws and change policies through the initiative process. Only 21 percent thought it was a "bad thing."

Voters' support reflects their confidence that they make better decisions than the governor and Legislature. Sixty percent of the voters thought that the electorate "probably" made better public policy decisions. Yet voters do not want too many propositions on the ballot. Nearly 60 percent said there were too many propositions. The survey also found that nearly four out of five likely voters thought citizens' initiatives were "too complicated and confusing" for them to determine the effect. So, despite the popular support for making fiscal decisions through direct appeal to the state's voters, the initiative cannot ever be a complete substitute for legislative and gubernatorial involvement. The public's involvement in fiscal decisions is limited by several factors.

The electorate cannot give direct voice to their opinions or interests outside of the regularly scheduled primary and general elections. Because elections typically are held in even-numbered years, the public provides its opinions episodically.

Even if they could provide some timely decisions, voters are unlikely to make sustainable decisions on the thousands of fiscal issues considered during the budget process. To the extent fiscal issues must be resolved in an iterative process, such as that afforded by the legislative budget process, propositions can supplement but not replace the current budget process. The state's annual budget requires consideration of thousands of issues. The propositions tend to deal with a very small percentage of these decisions. Propositions tend to address single programs and a limited number of decisions.

Nor is it likely that a proposition can sufficiently simplify the number of decisions or complexity of fiscal issues that must be decided to eliminate the need for legislative or executive involvement in fiscal management. Government programs, like other complex human endeavors, generally require active management. To remain effective and efficient, personnel and service objectives must be regularly assessed and adjusted. Few propositions can be written with sufficient precision to ensure that programs can be run without management's direct involvement. Nor can a single proposition anticipate how the state's finances and demographics change and affect policy. No proposition attempting to direct state spending, irrespective of how carefully drafted, can fully specify the circumstances under which the state will function in the future. Given the complexity of state finances, no initiative's language—no matter how contingent or specific—can anticipate state fiscal conditions. So, voters rely on the legislative and executive branches to set and manage most aspects of fiscal policy.

When voters rely on the governor and Legislature to set most fiscal policy, that policy is embodied in the annual budget document. But the budget document itself provides a limited means for making fiscal decisions or managing state finances. When the governor proposes the budget in the second week of January, his staff forwards a great amount of information to the legislative budget committees—schedules, explanations, justifications, and spreadsheets—providing minute detail about the basis for the numbers listed in the budget bill. While the detail justifies changes to the state's annual spending plan, the budget bill itself provides scant information.

The Limits of Using the Budget Bill

The budget bill itself, which is a list of appropriations following a limited format, is intended to provide a uniform description of each of thousands of appropriations for all kinds of state programs. It lists the department, appropriation, and the source of funding (that is, whether the appropriation will be paid for out of the General Fund or some special fund). It cannot provide any information about how the Legislature intends for the appropriation to be managed or the policies pursued with the appropriation. As such, the budget functions more as a summary of all the supporting material forwarded as part of the budget.

The bill may contain some "control" language that attempts to limit the use of or otherwise direct the amount appropriated. Control language is adopted by the Legislature to express legislative intent for the use of funds. So, if the Legislature wants to appropriate $5 million to the Superintendent of Public Instruction to develop curriculum, it may add to the superintendent's main appropriation and add language that attempts to direct the funds to the curriculum effort. However, the control language, like an appropriation, is subject to a governor's veto. Governors have vetoed control language when they signed the budget, thereby repealing legislative directives. Consequently, legislative attempts to direct spending will be achieved only through executive acquiescence and negotiation.

The state constitution also circumscribes how much the budget bill can be used to set policy. It limits the bill to making appropriations and prohibits the bill from containing statutory provisions. So, while the bill can appropriate $1 million for upgrading campground facilities, it cannot change California law governing the use of fire pits at campsites.

Even if the constitution did not limit its scope, the budget bill cannot accommodate the mass of detail required to specify all the management and policy issues assumed as part of the budget. For example, it cannot list the number of positions to be filled, or specify who should fill them. The Legislature also faces a delicate problem in trying to use the budget to change executive management practices. To the extent legislators want to change or direct how a department uses its appropriation, irrespective of level, the budget bill is an inadequate tool.

The Legislature Limits Its Ability to Set Fiscal Policy

In addition to the physical limits of the budget bill, the process used to construct the budget diminishes legislative control. The current procedures and protocols employed by the Legislature in negotiating the budget limit the Legislature's effectiveness in implementing and managing fiscal policy.

Power of the First Draft Undermines Legislative Control

As described in Chapter 1, the Legislature waits for the governor to propose the January budget. After the legislative analyst submits a long analysis of the governor's proposal, the Legislature begins its 10-week review of the proposal, typically in early March. Later in the year, when the governor proposes the May Revision with its potentially major changes in state spending, the Legislature again uses the governor's proposal as a point of departure when crafting a budget. In the case of the May Revision, the subcommittees are so pressed to complete their review of the revision before budget deadlines that they invariably adopt most of the governor's revision. By relying so heavily on the governor's budget proposals—and in other less-visible ways—the Legislature generally defers to the governor during the budget process.

It defers in part because the governor has more resources to devote to developing the details of the budget. However, by using the governor's budget proposals as the basis of its own budget deliberations, the Legislature gives the governor enormous influence over the terms of the budget debate. How much revenue is available for discretionary programs? Which programs will receive the discretionary revenue? The Legislature allows the governor to make the initial proposal by which all alternatives are reviewed. In short, it gives to the governor the "power of the first draft."

The power of the first draft has substantive and practical implications. By starting with the January proposal, the Legislature must take an action to change the governor's budget or the budget bill will remain as proposed. If the Legislature proposes to delete a provision, then that department or interest subject to the deletion can identify precisely what and by how much it has lost. When the Legislature defers to the January plan, its inertia benefits the governor's proposal.

In a typical budget, the Legislature changes a small number of appropriations recommended by the governor in the January or May budget proposals. This suggests that the Legislature either defers to the governor's proposals or feels unable to resist them.

Is the governor's proposal always and consistently preferable to legislative alternatives? Those occasions when the Legislature ignored the governor's January budget suggests how powerful the governor's initial draft of the budget can be in influencing subsequent decisions. One example occurred in 2002, when the full Senate budget committee struck all the governor's discretionary augmentations from the governor's January proposals. Before asking the subcommittees to consider the governor's budget, the full committee deleted $2 billion worth of discretionary spending proposals. The budget committee chair, Senator Steve Peace, authorized the subcommittee chairs to consider restoring the governor's proposals or use the funding for their own priorities. In few cases did the subcommittee chairs restore the governor's proposals. Instead, they spent the $2 billion on other augmentations, thereby reflecting a different spending priority than the governor's. Because the full committee struck Davis's own original proposals, the subcommittee chairs felt empowered to establish their own priorities because the governor's budget had been stripped of the governor's priorities before they began deliberations. This example suggests that when the Legislature uses the governor's first draft of the budget, the Legislature will defer to the governor's spending priorities.

Trailer Bills Undermine the Legislature's Own Policy Development Process

The state constitution prevents the Legislature from adopting policy changes in the budget bill. This prohibition appears to limit budget negotiations to financing current law provisions. By limiting the scope of negotiations, the prohibition would discourage logrolling, a negotiating practice that would tie nonbudget issues to passage of the essential budget. It would also encourage the Legislature and governor to seek policy changes through the Legislature's policy development process. The Legislature has a series of committees with policy expertise that are charged with hearing and shaping legislation.

In practice, however, the Legislature and governor seek major policy changes as a part of the budget process. As budget negotiations close, policy changes requiring amendments to statutory law are indirectly tied to passage of the budget bill. These bills, known as trailer bills because their passage "trails" the budget, are passed by the Legislature at the same time as the budget bill itself. By making the bills contemporaneous, the Legislature makes the budget bill contingent on the success of trailer bills.

The use of trailer bills to make new policy can be extensive or limited, depending on budget and political circumstances. Sometimes the use of trailer bills is justified as necessary to ensure that spending levels are consistent with the provisions of the budget bill. For example, when the Legislature seeks to reduce certain statutory benefits (such as a cost-of-living adjustment for welfare), it needs a budget trailer bill to cut the benefit. In recent years, the Legislature and governor have sought many trailer bills, and many of the changes are not necessary to implement the budget bill.

Most often, trailer bills are not reviewed by the Legislature's policy committees. Nor are the trailer bills subject to the kind of policy scrutiny and hearing that other policy changes undergo in the Legislature's policy development process. By using trailer bills to pursue policy changes unrelated to the budget, the Legislature and governor expect to use the budget process to expedite and streamline the passage of statutory law change. While going around its own process may be expedient, it also serves to undermine the Legislature's own policy experts. The construction of policy without due consideration can lead to poorly constructed statutory law, and adoption of legislation with ill-considered effects.

Process Does Not Foster Sufficient Interhouse Collaboration

From January 10 until the May Revision, there is little opportunity for collaboration among the five parties to the budget negotiation. From mid-January through March 1, legislative staff review the governor's budget proposal and wait for the publication of the analyst's review, which is delivered in late February. From March 1 until the end of May, each house independently reviews the budget. Members and their subcommittee staff may discuss budget options with their counterparts in the opposite house, but there is no opportunity for joint review and action. The minority party members and staff rarely have a chance to influence the product of the subcommittee.

Nor is the governor engaged in the subcommittee process. The governor's representative at the subcommittee meetings, the staff of the Department of Finance, cannot negotiate on the governor's behalf. They are strictly limited to supporting the governor's budget as proposed in January.

There may be informal discussion between the houses and between the caucuses, but there is little opportunity for collaborative action. The subcommittee review tends to reflect the perspective and interests of the majority party, most often the Democrats. At the hearings the discussion and review includes the minority party but there is little opportunity or incentive to develop a consensus document that reflects bipartisan interests.

As a result, the subcommittee effort, as it tends to reflect the work of the majority party in the house, yields a product of slight practical value for purposes of securing sufficient votes among the minority or the opposite house. Nor does it reflect amendments that will secure gubernatorial approval. As a result, for most of the subcommittee process the limitations of the current process make negotiation, much less consensus, very unlikely. In practice, there may be no budget discussion among the four legislative parties and governor until June. Negotiations with the governor, Republicans, and indeed the Democratic members from the other house do not begin until the conference committee begins its work, typically in late May or early June.

After the May Revision, There Is Insufficient Time for Review of Key Budget Decisions

The governor releases the May Revision, which often includes major policy changes, on or around May 14. In order to complete the subcommittee review and begin the budget conference committee around the Memorial Day holiday, the subcommittees must finish their review of the revision and take actions within two weeks of the revision's release. Compared to the review of the January proposal, the consideration of the May Revision is much more slight, cursory, and hasty. Rarely is there time for sufficient consideration and public testimony of the policy changes.

Immediately after completing their work, the subcommittees submit their product to the budget conference committee. The Legislature invests a great deal of responsibility in this forum for crafting a budget compromise among the five parties to the negotiation. Unlike the subcommittee process, the conference committee does not take public testimony. In this forum, the Department of Finance and the four caucuses all have a place in the negotiations. They typically have two weeks to complete their review of the subcommittee work, and develop a compromise acceptable to all parties to the negotiation.

When the conference committee cannot complete a compromise, it relies on direct negotiations between the legislative leadership and the governor. When the "Big Five" complete their deal, the compromise is quickly written and rushed through the two houses for delivery to the governor.

At the completion of the six-month review process, the compromise—sometimes finished in private negotiations—is often rushed to each house. There is little or no opportunity for the legislative members, the press, or the public to review the details of proposed final deal before the legislative consideration. This is because there is rarely a published budget bill. The language of any accompanying legislation also tends to be unavailable in published form.

Fiscal Policy Is Not Set Exclusively in the Budget

The Legislature's power to appropriate is an exclusive constitutional franchise and potentially a source of power to influence policy. To exercise its fiscal powers, the Legislature must take a specific action. To make a valid appropriation, the Legislature must adopt a spending bill—signed by the governor—which specifies a department, a purpose, and an amount for the appropriation. Though the Legislature typically makes these appropriations in the budget bill, it may make the appropriation in other legislation as well. The exclusive power to authorize spending confers enormous responsibility to the Legislature to ensure that spending is prudent, conforms to statutory law, and is consistent with legislative policy. By withholding an appropriation or by imposing conditions on the way a department spends, the Legislature can extend its power over statutory entities.

If the Legislature withholds an appropriation, it can prevent the governor from taking an action. If it directs spending to a specific program, it can direct the action of government. In recent years, however, whether because of convenience or disinterest, the Legislature has diminished its control in the budget process. Its budgetary deferral has become routine and habitual.

Outside the budget process, the Legislature may pursue many goals simultaneously. These other goals, such as expanding important programs or reducing taxes, can be seen as being in competition with limiting financial control. To the extent the Legislature pursues these other goals, it may be willing to let fiscal control be reduced in favor of achieving these other goals.

In recent years, as the Legislature has delegated major financial decisions to the governor and allowed the executive branch to exercise greater fiscal control. In December 2003, Governor Schwarzenegger's first director of finance, Donna Arduin, notified the Legislature that the administration would increase appropriations to immunize local governments for losses associated with a reduction in local revenues. This $3 billion allocation was in direct contradiction to language approved in the Budget Act, and "represent[ed] a major revision to legislative policy," according to the legislative analyst.[2] When the Legislature returned to Sacramento in January 2004, it did not attempt to stop the governor's unilateral appropriation. (It did pass—much later in the year—a bill to authorize spending the money the governor asserted could be spent pursuant to an emergency executive order.)

This billion-dollar allocation is remarkable because it shows that the Legislature is willing to acquiesce to the governor's fiscal decisions on major policy. Nor is it a singular example. About the same time that the administration was making an appropriation without legislative authority, it raised nearly $2 billion in taxes without a legislative vote.[3]

Adopting Vague Law Increases Administrative Discretion over Fiscal Decisions

The Legislature provides the executive with additional administrative discretion over fiscal matters when it assigns broad or vague statutory responsibilities to departments. For example, in 2006, the Legislature attempted to create a new program for managing the release of greenhouse gases. The bill, Assembly Bill 32 (Nunez), required the Air Resources Board to adopt administrative practices for regulating private industry. The bill, a mere 17 pages long, outlined policy direc-

---

[2] Elizabeth Hill, "Deficiencies: Rethinking How to Address Unexpected Expenses," *Perspectives and Issues* (February 2004): 143.

[3] John Decker, "Resolving Differences and Crafting Compromise," *Governing California*, ed. Jerry Lubenow (Berkeley, Calif.: IGS Press, 2004).

tion about how to implement the Legislature's intent. It provided little detail about how the Legislature expected the administration to start up or run the regulatory program. So the Air Resources Board and other executive agencies have wide discretion to implement the bill's provisions.

The bill also gave the air board authority to assess fees to implement the provisions of the bill. Before imposing the fees, the board is to assess its needs and determine a fee structure to fully finance the provisions of the bill. The bill provides for no consultation with the Legislature prior to imposing the fee. As the fee could apply to a wide range of commercial and industrial businesses, this fee could be imposed on a great number of payers. Though there are differing interpretations about how AB 32 will be implemented, the on-going administrative costs could exceed $50 million annually.[4] These fees could be structured and levied without any legislative involvement, pursuant to the provisions of the bill.

By delegating both the regulatory and fiscal policy decisions, AB 32 illustrates the hazards for the Legislature when it delegates broad decisions to departments. AB 32 is not unique. A review of state regulatory law identifies many policy areas where the Legislature has transferred major policy decisions to the administration. While the financing of these programs is generally subject to an appropriation, unlike AB 32, the use of any legislative appropriation becomes a prerogative of the executive.

The Legislature also defers to the executive when it fails to appropriate sufficient funds to cover a department's entire statutory responsibilities. When insufficient funding is appropriated, a department uses its discretion to comply with only those laws that it deems appropriate. For several years, in part as a response to the state's chronic budget deficits, the Legislature has underfunded programs and departments. Consider, for example, that the Department of Fish and Game has broad statutory responsibilities to protect and manage the state's natural habitats in near-shore ocean areas and on land. To fully meet this statutory obligation, the department's budget would have to be quadrupled, at least. Being short of a full appropriation, the department is selective in how it attempts to protect the state's natural habitat. It ignores some statutory mandates and partially implements the rest.

Increasingly, the Legislature copes with complex policy issues by adopting vague law. The executive uses this vagueness by broadening its administrative control over program implementation and finances.

Spending without Legislative Oversight

The Budget Act provides an appropriation for a single year. By limiting the duration of the appropriation, the Legislature reserves to itself the opportunity to review the appropriation in later years. The annual review allows the Legislature

---

[4] Legislative Analyst's Office, "Implementation of AB 32" Analysis of the Budget, 2008, (Sacramento, Calif.: Legislative Analyst's Office, 2008) B29.

to adjust the spending to reflect the performance of departments. The Legislature may withhold a portion of an appropriation until a department demonstrates that it has improved its performance. Or the Legislature can adjust appropriations to reflect changing fiscal conditions. It can reduce spending when revenues underperform.

An annual appropriation requires an annual action; a continuous appropriation does not. For this reason, departments prefer to be exempt from this annual scrutiny. To avoid annual budget review, departments may seek a permanent appropriation that does not depend on subsequent passage of the annual budget bill. There are many ways to construct this automatic appropriation in statute, they are collectively known as a "continuous appropriation." The statute can appropriate every year at a certain date (like the start of the fiscal year) or under certain conditions.

One such continuous appropriation allocates $15 million annually from the surplus revenue derived from deposits on recycled bottles. The appropriation is to local conservation corps to conduct recycling outreach, promotion, and service. The Legislature imposes no scrutiny on the use of this $15 million. Neither the governor's budget nor the Department of Conservation's website provides any detail on the annual use of these funds.

So powerful is the value of a continuous appropriation that the interested parties will fight to protect it. In 2006 the Senate Appropriations Committee attempted to repeal the continuous appropriation and require the $15 million to be appropriated annually. Though the committee generally sought limitations and repeals of continuous appropriations, the state Department of Conservation and the environmental lobbyists lobbied to retain the continuous appropriation. Finally, the local corps chapter called committee members to remind them how they spent their share of the $15 million. In the end, the corps retained its continuous appropriation.

The Department of Finance estimated that of the $103 billion spent from the General Fund in 2007–08, only $71.5 billion (69 percent) was appropriated through the Budget Act. Another $24.7 billion (23 percent) was appropriated by statutory law. The balance was appropriated by constitutional provision or other means. At a minimum, this suggests that roughly 30 percent of the budget is outside the provisions of the annual Budget Act.

Neither the legislative analyst nor legislative counsel tracks the instances of the granted continuous appropriations. Without a specific accounting for these appropriations, the Legislature will find it hard to monitor the use of these appropriations made outside of the budget. As such, continuous appropriations rob the Legislature of the opportunity for examining the ongoing performance of programs.

Making Policy within Fiscal Complexity

The state's fiscal structure supports the provision of a broad range of services. Many of these programs and services are so large that they defy easy comprehension or administrative control. There are many ways to modify the state's fiscal structure and make policy: directly through the electoral process, through the legislative process, or by administrative practice. In the midst of this broad access and complexity, the Legislature and governor must collaborate to authorize spending, adjust taxes, or make "off budget" decisions. They must simultaneously consider the fiscal and political implications on the state's fiscal condition.

Because the state's fiscal structure and dynamics are too often shaped by circumstances outside the context of the annual budget deliberations, the Legislature cannot rely on the budget instrument itself to direct policy. To increase its fiscal control and reassert its ability to influence policy, the Legislature will need to consider how it reviews and acts on fiscal choices. It may have to consider when it uses its fiscal powers. For example: Would it be willing to change its procedures to devote more time to the May Revision? To achieve policy goals, would it withhold appropriations or limit administrative discretion?

Chapter 3

Financing the Budget

Governor Pete Wilson was not shy about raising taxes in 1991. In his view, the tax code, as it read when he took office, did not generate enough revenue to finance all the state's spending commitments. Although his first priority was to cut government spending, Wilson believed it was unrealistic to expect the state to balance the budget by relying exclusively on spending cuts. In his first year in office, he proposed raising taxes by almost 20 percent, or $8 billion, and worked hard to build support for the idea. On June 16, he saw the fruits of his efforts when five Republicans joined Democrats in the Senate to pass legislation raising taxes by over $4 billion. But Assembly Republicans were less sanguine about the need for tax increases. When they considered the Senate tax package later that same day, not a single Assembly Republican voted for it. Assemblyman Ross Johnson, the minority leader, urged his colleagues to hold out for greater spending cuts *in lieu* of the taxes. Wilson was openly contemptuous of the Assembly Republicans for what he considered a lack of courage, telling the *Los Angeles Times* that

> . . . the easiest possible thing in politics is to say "no" to taxes and let other people vote for them. It doesn't require anything. It allows you to demagogue rather easily."[1]

When asked by the *San Francisco Chronicle* whether he would pressure recalcitrant members of his own party, Wilson said he was prepared to twist, and if necessary break, their arms to get the increased taxes.[2] It took a lot of twisting.

---

[1] George Skelton, "Wilson, Leaders Fail Budget's Political Lesson," *Los Angeles Times*, July 7, 1991, A1.

[2] Robert B. Gunnison and Greg Lucas, "Wilson Says Budget Has Enough Votes," *San Francisco Chronicle*, June 18, 1991, A1.

Not until June 28, as the start of the fiscal year approached, did Assembly Republicans begin voting for the tax increases. By the time Wilson signed the 1991 budget on July 16, nine Assembly Republicans voted to raise taxes by $6.1 billion. The month-long battle scarred all the participants. Johnson, having fought hard to prevent the tax increases, lost his leadership position to the coalition of Republican assemblymembers who had voted to increase taxes with Wilson and the Democratic majority.

The 1991 legislation raised all of the most visible taxes, including the income, sales, vehicle license, cigarette, and alcohol taxes. The tax increases were contained in six pieces of legislation, and were a significant part of a 16-bill package adopted as part of the negotiated 1991 budget deal. Some of the tax increases were intended to be permanent, including the increases in the vehicle, cigarette, and alcohol taxes. Other parts of these bills were intended to be temporary, as the provisions were written to expire after a few years. For example, though the package included an increase in the tax rate for the state's wealthiest taxpayers, the increase sunsetted automatically in the mid 1990s. So, two years after the Legislature raised taxes by an unprecedented amount, about 40 percent of the $6 billion tax increase expired, having been enacted as temporary tax increases. By 1996–97, all the changes enacted as part of the 1991 tax package were generating only $1.3 billion on an ongoing basis.

Then, starting in 1994, the Legislature adopted subsequent legislation that on a net basis further reduced taxes in each of the next seven years. Governor Wilson and his successor, Gray Davis, signed legislation reducing taxes on personal income, corporations, and vehicles. The cumulative effect of these reductions was so large that, when Governor Arnold Schwarzenegger proposed his first budget in 2003, the annual revenue gains of the 1991 tax increases had been fully offset by the subsequent tax reductions.

This chapter places those intervening tax-law changes in their fiscal and historical context. Which classes of taxpayers have paid more since 1991? Why did taxes fall so dramatically between 1992 and 2001? To consider these changes, this chapter first presents an overview of the tax structure in place on January 1, 2008, to detail how the state generates over $100 billion in revenue every year. It then looks at how the legislation changed the tax structure between 1991 and 2008 by considering each tax change in its context by discussing the tax changes in the year they were adopted. A subsequent chapter evaluates whether the state is generating sufficient revenue.

Tax Structure: How Does California Finance Its Budget?

California's tax system is vast. In the broadest terms, the state expects to collect revenues from general taxes totaling about $95.3 billion in 2007–08, about $2,528 for every person in the state. All state levies (including general taxes, special taxes, and other charges) would generate revenue of $111.8 billion—

$2,964 per capita—in the same year.[3] Though the state generates revenue from many sources, the personal income tax and the sales tax produce 69 percent of all revenues.[4] Because of the relative importance of these two taxes, the governor and Legislature can have the greatest impact on revenues when they make changes in these two taxes. Small adjustments in their tax base or rates can have a big impact on the state's revenues. A five percent sales tax reduction would have cut taxes by $1.6 billion in 2007–08. By way of comparison, if the state had eliminated the entire tax on alcoholic beverages, the change would reduce taxes by less than $350 million.

The state has two other major revenue sources, the corporation and the motor vehicle fuel taxes, which respectively generated about 8.8 percent and 4.0 percent of state revenues. The corporation tax is a tax on business activity and the fuel tax is essentially the gas tax.

All the state's other revenue sources, which when combined, generated about one-tenth of total state revenues, derive from a plethora of taxes, fees, and charges. None of these other revenue streams generated more than two percent of total revenues. Only three generated more than $1 billion annually, and none generated more than $3 billion. They are taxes on vehicle registration and insurance policies. While most Californians are aware of the state's levy of "sin taxes" on cigarettes and alcohol, each one of these other revenue streams represents less than two percent of all state revenues. Indeed, the income tax generates more revenue in just three weeks than do any of these minor exactions during an entire year.

Describing Taxes

Tax revenues are the product of the tax rate and the tax base. In recent years, the tax rates have been widely debated. For example, in the statewide election held in November 2004, the voters approved a higher tax rate for the state's wealthiest taxpayers. But the tax rate that received the greatest attention in recent years has been the rate imposed on vehicles. In 1996, the rate was two percent of the depreciated value of the car or truck. Between 1997 and 2003, the Legislature and Governors Wilson and Davis labored over how much to reduce the tax rate. The rate was a topic in Governor Wilson's last year and throughout Governor Davis's governorship. It played a role in the gubernatorial recall ending Davis's tenure.

In 1997, the state cut the rate by 25 percent, and dropped it again in 1998 so that vehicle owners paid only .67 percent on their car's value—a nearly 75 percent drop in tax rates. In the face of large budget deficits, the Legislature considered whether to raise the tax rate back to two percent in 2002. The legislation, which

---

[3] Department of Finance, "Schedule 2," *Governor's Budget 2009* (Sacramento, Calif.).
  [4] *Ibid.*

could have raised annual revenues, could pass the Legislature only if it were approved by two-thirds of the members in the Assembly and Senate. Instead of directly raising taxes, the Legislature authorized the director of the Department of Finance to raise the tax when necessary. Through an odd quirk in the law, this change passed with a simple majority vote of each house. When in 2003 Steve Peace, the finance director, used this authority to raise the tax rate, the tax increase became a topic in the gubernatorial recall. After succeeding Davis in the recall, Arnold Schwarzenegger's first gubernatorial action was to lower the car tax rate.

Though tax rates have received a great deal of attention, the tax base—who and what is taxed—is as important in determining what taxes are paid. In the case of the income tax and the corporation tax, taxpayers use deductions (reductions in the amount of taxable income) and credits (reductions in their computed tax) to reduce their tax liability. For example, taxpayers may deduct from their taxable income the amount they contribute in support of recognized charities. In 2004,[5] 5.3 million California taxpayers itemized contributing $28.4 billion to religious organizations, governmental bodies, nonprofit service groups, and the like. By deducting these contributions from their taxes, taxpayers reduced their state tax payments by $1.4 billion.

While rates have been highly visible on statewide ballots during the Davis and Schwarzenegger administrations, the tax base often has a greater effect on what is taxed, who pays, and when the tax is due. Discussions about the tax base are often freighted with political nuance. What one critic denounces as a "tax break" may be a supporter's "incentive." A "tax loophole" may also be a necessary tax provision to ensure "equal treatment" among taxpayers.

To find neutral language for a discussion of exemptions from the tax base, public finance economists use the phrase "tax expenditures," which implies an equivalence between benefits provided through the tax code and through direct spending in the budget. For example, the charitable deduction reduced taxes by about $1.4 billion. Using the economists' formulation, the tax loss associated with the charitable gift deduction is equivalent to a $1.4 billion state expenditure on behalf of these charities. By thinking of the tax effects in this way, the governor and Legislature can weigh the effectiveness of distributing $1.4 billion through a tax reduction and a direct expenditure. Perhaps allowing individuals to contribute to their favorite charity—without the intervention of elected officials—ensures the contributions reflect the best use of taxpayers' desires and earnings.

It is certain that the Legislature would not allocate revenues to the same groups or in the same amount as do individuals and corporations. Not all the $28.4 billion that Californians donated benefited Californians or California-based organizations. Because California's tax code authorizes a tax deduction for any federally qualified arts organization, the contributions could have been to any arts organization in the United States, including the Metropolitan Opera in New York. Surely, if the Legislature were allocating $1.4 billion in tax revenue, it would not send a dime to The Met.

---

[5] Franchise Tax Board, *Income Tax Expenditures*, December 2007, 62.

Who is better able to distribute the $1.4 billion? Alas, the economists' formulation, while a helpful conceptual framework, provides little guidance on the merit of expenditures. For example, the tax deduction could be said to allow the state to leverage an increase in the private support for social purposes by over $28.4 billion at a cost of only $1.4 billion, thereby increasing the amount of private resources the state directs to social purposes. But this analysis implies that all $28.4 billion was donated *as a result of* California's tax deduction. This cannot be so: Some taxpayers would contribute without a state tax deduction. The federal tax code provides a larger tax reduction for similar contributions, so the federal tax credit provides a larger incentive to give. California's smaller deduction often would have an incremental, and not a determinative, effect on how much is contributed. There is no current analysis able to calibrate the value of the deduction and the contributions.

Even if the discussion of tax "expenditures" does not come to a clear analytical resolution, identifying their "cost" helps contextualize deductions and credits. The Department of Finance estimates that for those expenditures whose value they could estimate the expenditures reduced taxes by about $49 billion in 2008–09.[6] If all the expenditures were repealed, tax rates could be reduced by about 40 percent and the tax system would generate the same amount of revenue.

Below is a brief summary of the state's major taxes, with a description of the tax rates, base, and expenditures.

Personal Income Tax Is the Largest Single Revenue Source

The state's most productive revenue source, the personal income tax, accounts for over 40 cents of every dollar collected by the state. The state levies the tax on the net income of individuals with the rate increasing as incomes rise so that higher income taxpayers pay a higher tax rate.

As the largest revenue source, the personal income tax is subject to some of the greatest scrutiny by the public and policymakers. Often, the public's discussion of tax issues centers on whether the state's wealthiest taxpayers pay their "fair share." At the statewide election held on November 3, 1992, the California Tax Reform Association placed before the voters a proposal to raise taxes on the state's wealthiest taxpayers. The association's executive director, Lenny Goldberg, wrote in the *Voter's Pamphlet* that the income tax increase was justified because, "During the 1980s the top one percent of Californians saw their after-tax incomes rise by over 75 percent, while the average income of the bottom 80 percent was unchanged." In response, opponents said the higher tax rates "would ultimately hit middle and lower income families because businesses would be forced to cut jobs or increase consumer prices." The arguments are not mutually exclusive, and both sides can be correct about the effects of tax changes.

---

[6] Department of Finance. *Tax Expenditures Report 2008–09*, (Sacramento, Calif.), 4.

While there may be a growing income discrepancy between the state's most wealthy and everyone else, raising taxes on the rich could reduce jobs and raise prices. Californians may be genuinely conflicted about the extent to which wealthier taxpayers should pay a greater share of the tax burden. So in 1992, Californians defeated the measure to raise the top income tax rates, but approved a similar tax rate change in 2004 when the proceeds of the tax increase were earmarked for mental health programs. Proposition 63 on the November 2004 ballot passed with 54 percent of the vote.

The debate about "taxing the rich" tends to focus on raising tax rates on the high-income taxpayers. It does not tend to address ways of expanding the tax base to generate revenue from high-income taxpayers.

The Income Tax Base

Though it may not be the subject of the same kind of public debate or statewide elections as tax rates, the income tax base is broad and dynamic. Most income tax revenue derives from levies on annual compensation, as income from wages and salaries account for nearly two-thirds of the revenue generated by the tax. Income from sales of capital investments accounted for one-eighth. Other taxable sources are income from interest and dividends, rents and royalties, and partnerships. Each of these lesser sources accounted for less than six percent of the revenue in 2005 tax year.[7] Figure 3.1 graphically describes the state's income tax base in 2005.[8]

The base can change from year to year, as taxpayers receive different kinds of income. The most dramatic, though temporary, change in the income tax base was associated with a steep increase in the amount of taxable capital gains for Californians for the five years beginning in 1996. Until 2000, Californians received large increases in their income when they sold their stock holdings. The values of certain companies, particularly in the high technology ("Dot com") stocks, had appreciated very rapidly in the early 1990s. As Californians sold these stocks, they realized large income gains relative to the price they paid for the stock

Though the state has a broad income tax base, the tax code provides for many credits, deductions, and exemptions. The Department of Finance estimates that those provisions reduced income taxes by $33.4 billion in 2006–07. Over half of these were associated with employer-paid benefits and property ownership. Figure

---

[7] The California Franchise Tax Board publishes a statistical abstract each year detailing the income and corporations taxes. The latest available data relate to the tax returns filed in Spring 2005, and cover the 2005 tax year.

[8] California Franchise Tax Board, *Annual Report* (Sacramento, Calif.), 2006, 20.

Figure 3.1. Source of Income, by Major Category, Personal Income Tax, 2005 Tax Year

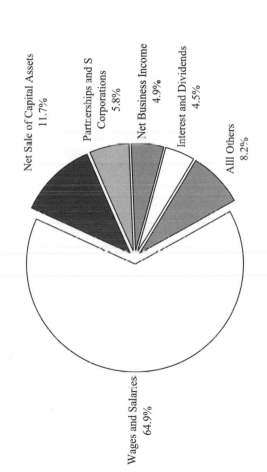

Net Sale of Capital Assets
11.7%

Partnerships and S
Corporations
5.8%

Net Business Income
4.9%

Interest and Dividends
4.5%

Alll Others
8.2%

Wages and Salaries
64.9%

3.2 displays the relative value of the major income tax expenditures, and the categories are described in detail below.[9]

Taxpayers may reduce costs for property—and especially residential property—ownership in four ways by taking advantage of the provisions of the income the tax code. Taken together, these exemptions reduced income taxes by the greatest amount of any type of tax preferences. The home-mortgage interest deduction is the largest tax break for which many individual taxpayers qualify each year. About 8.2 million taxpayers claimed it and reduced their taxes by $5.0 billion.[10] It is available only to homeowners who have loans. Its annual value for the individual homeowner varies depending on the taxpayer's particular situation, including the size of the home loan, the amount of interest paid and the homeowner's tax bracket. The tax deduction is generally justified as encouraging homeownership, even though it does not discriminate between a mortgage of a one-bedroom condominium serving as a primary residence and a three-bedroom vacation home.

The code also authorizes homeowners to realize the appreciated value of their homes without incurring a tax liability. The gain is "income" to the taxpayer, but the law allows her to deduct this income from her taxes, thereby reducing taxes by a total of $4.2 billion in 2006–07.

All property owners—including homeowners—may also benefit from two other major expenditures. They may deduct the value of their payments for local property taxes. In 2006–07, 8.2 million taxpayers[11] claimed this deduction for a tax savings of $1.3 billion. Individual taxpayers benefit from another tax expenditure less frequently, but its application has large tax consequences. At those times when property transfers to an heir, the property's value is revised up to the fair market value at the time of the decedent's death. This change, known as "step-up in basis," allows heirs to shelter any appreciation in property value that occurred during the decedent's life. State law conforms with federal treatment of these gains and reduced state taxes by about $3.9 billion.

The second-largest group of income tax expenditures is the employer-paid benefits, accounting for about one-quarter of the total value of all income tax expenditures in 2006–07. They include contributions to health plans ($2.9 billion), to pension plans ($4.1 billion), and to life insurance plans ($97.0 million). By exempting these contributions, the state provides an economic incentive for both employers and employees to make insurance and pension benefits a part of their compensation.[12]

---

[9] Department of Finance, "Table 1," *Tax Expenditure Report 2008–09* (Sacramento, Calif.).

[10] Department of Finance, *Tax Expenditure Report 2008–09* (Sacramento, Calif.) 12.

[11] *Ibid.*, 12.

[12] The exemption for contributions to pension plans could be considered a deferral of taxation, as pension benefits are subject to the full tax when they are paid to the pensioner. The tax rate paid at a later date may be lower or higher for the individual taxpayer, depending both on the taxpayer's comparative taxable income and the statewide tax rates in effect.

Figure 3.2. Share of Major Tax Expenditures, Personal Income Tax, 2006–07

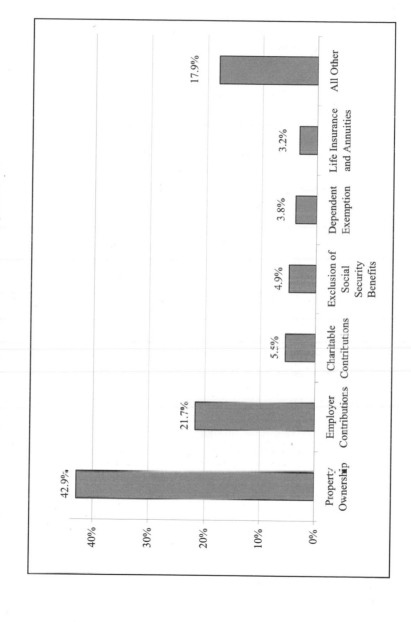

The state exempts the payment of certain "insurance" payments, including federal Social Security benefits and life insurance benefits. In 2006–07, about 1.8 million taxpayers[13] claimed the Social Security exemption for a tax savings of about $1.6 billion. Taxpayers also received tax savings from the exemption as beneficiaries of life insurance, for a savings of nearly $1.1 billion. "Insurance" exemptions accounted for nearly 8.1 percent of all income tax expenditures.

Taxpayers with dependents may claim an income tax credit of up to $294 per dependent in 2007. The credit is nonrefundable, so taxpayers with low tax liabilities may not qualify for its full amount. The value of the credit is phased-out for high-income taxpayers (in 2007, the credit began phasing out for joint filers with adjusted gross incomes exceeding $310,000). About 3.1 million taxpayers claim at least one dependent each year for a tax savings of about $1.3 billion.

The law also provides a refundable credit for taxpayers who must buy care for their dependents. The taxpayer calculates the amount of the credit on a variable percentage of actual expenses, where the percentage is inversely related to income. The maximum annual value of the credit is capped at a little over $900. Over 600,000 taxpayers claim this credit annually, for a tax savings in excess of $160 million.[14]

Aside from these exemptions and deductions, most other income is subject to the state's income tax. The income tax system is often referred to as a "progressive" system, as the rate at which income is taxed rises with income. A progressive rate system, intended to make taxpayers with higher incomes pay a larger share of their income in taxes than do taxpayers at lower incomes, increases the tax load on taxpayers as their income rises. In 2008, the rates start at a low of one percent and progress to a high of 10.3 percent. This "progressive" increase in the tax rate can be contrasted to the flat rate on the sales tax. (In the sales tax, the rate paid by each taxpayer is the same, irrespective of the taxpayer's income.) California's income tax system has been "progressive" since it was first levied in the 1930s.

Table 3.1 shows the tax brackets for the 2007 tax year for married taxpayers filing jointly. The income tax rate was one percent for all taxable income up to $13,654. Taxable income between $13,654 and $32,370 was subject to a two percent rate. The tax rate rose through similar income brackets for the upper rates. All taxable income above $1 million was taxed at the highest rate of 10.3 percent. The rates are applied to lower-income thresholds for single taxpayers or married persons filing separately. The rates vary by the filer's marital status to ensure that a married couple pays roughly the same tax for both partners' incomes as two unmarried people would pay separately.

State law adjusts the tax brackets annually for inflation using the California Consumer Price Index. Without indexing, taxpayers could be pushed into higher tax brackets even if their income is only growing at the rate of inflation and

---

[13] Department of Finance, *Tax Expenditure Report 2008–09* (Sacramento, Calif.), 15.
[14] Department of Finance, "Table 1," *Tax Expenditure Report 2008–09* (Sacramento, Calif.).

Table 3.1. Tax Brackets, Married Filing Jointly, 2007

Tax Rate	Taxable Income		
1.0	0	to	$ 13,654
2.0	$13,654	to	32,370
4.0	32,370	to	51,088
6.0	51,088	to	70,920
8.0	70,920	to	89,628
9.3	89,628	to	999,999
10.3	$1,000,000	and over	

therefore not giving them greater purchasing power. Indexing is an especially important protection for taxpayers when inflation rates are high, as they were in the late 1970s and early 1980s.

The progressive tax rate structure concentrates tax payments on a small percentage of all taxpayers.[15] Taxpayers with adjusted gross incomes of less than $30,000 constitute about 56.3 percent of all taxpayers, but pay less than one percent of the total income tax collected. At the other income extreme, taxpayers with adjusted gross incomes in excess of $99,999 are 13.6 percent of the returns and pay 83.0 percent of the tax. See Figure 3.3.

Another way to describe the effects of progressivity is to compare shares of income and shares of tax. As displayed in Figure 3.4, taxpayers with incomes above $100,000 have 56.5 percent of all income, but pay 83.0 percent of all tax. This difference becomes even more pronounced in the highest incomes.

Because of the progressivity, most other taxpayers pay a small portion of the total. By concentrating so much of the state's income tax load on the state's wealthiest taxpayers, the level of income tax receipts reflects the financial health and tax behavior of the richest Californians. When they experience a decline in taxable income, as happened in 2001, tax receipts will fall. But there are other implications. The wealthiest taxpayers have greater discretion for planning when they realize their California taxable income, allowing them to shift tax payments among tax years. For example, when these taxpayers shelter their income in tax-exempt investments before realizing their nonsalaried income, state income tax receipts will fall.

---

[15] Franchise Tax Board, *Annual Report 2006* (Sacramento, Calif.), B-2.

Figure 3.3. Comparison of Share of Tax Liability and Share of Taxpayers by Income Class, Personal Income Year, 2005 Tax Year

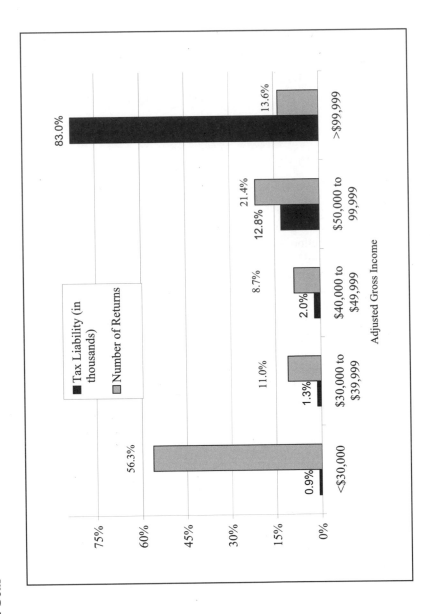

Figure 3.4. Comparison of Tax Liability and Adjusted Gross Income by Income Class, Personal Income Tax, 2005 Tax Year

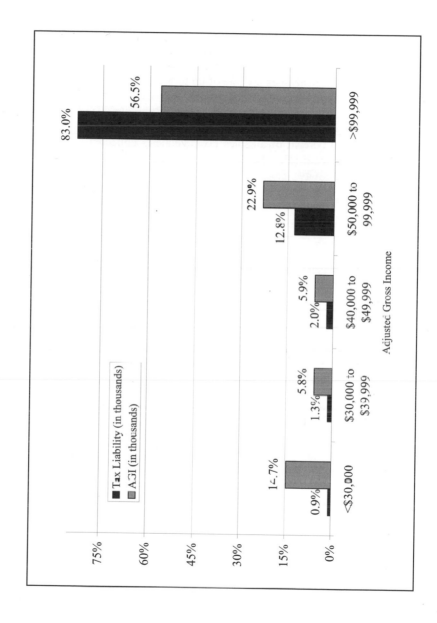

The Sales and Use Tax Is Primarily a Tax on Retail Transactions

The second largest revenue source, the sales and use tax, accounts for 24.5 percent of total revenue. The law imposes the tax on the final sales of tangible personal property. The state levies a permanent statewide sales tax rate and local governments may add onto the state sales tax base by as much as 3 percent, for a combined state/local sales tax rate of up to 8.75 percent. Though the state rate is applied evenly in all counties, variations in *local* tax efforts mean that the combined rate can vary from 7.25 percent to 8.75 percent. The Legislature also imposed a temporary additional one percent sales tax rate starting April 1, 2009.

About 70 percent of all sales tax revenue is collected at the retail level. In 2004–05, the retail sale of automobiles accounted for about 18.7 percent of all retail sales activity. Sales at service stations generated another 9.6 percent. Transactions at general and specialty stores accounted for 15.3 percent and 13.9 percent, respectively. Figure 3.5 displays the sources of sales tax revenue by type of business.[16]

The Sales Tax Base in Decline?

The Legislature may be concerned about the decline in the sales tax base. In a long-term and national trend, Americans are buying more services with their retail dollars than they did in the past. Instead of buying a lawnmower (which would be subject to the sales tax), more of our neighbors have gardening services (which is not subject to the sales tax). So, in 1945, consumers spent over 65 percent of their income on goods, and most of these goods transactions were subject to the sales tax. By 2002, consumers spent less than 45 percent[17] on goods. In the same period, the purchase of services rose from 45 percent to 65 percent. While consumers shift their buying patterns to the purchase of services, the sales tax base shrinks.

In California, taxing services could generate a large increase in sales tax revenue. For example, if the state were to tax waste collection services, it would generate $2 billion annually. It could generate $1 billion each from taxing repair services (predominately car repair) and trades (such as masonry, carpentry, and roofing). If the state were to tax entertainment (e.g., entrance to sporting events and movies) it could generate about $500 million. In 2007, the State Board of Equalization estimated that the tax base—if it were extended to services and

---

[16] State Board of Equalization, "Table 19," *Annual Report 2004–05* (Sacramento, Calif.).

[17] Ronald Snell, *New Realities in State Finance* (Boulder, Colo.: National Conference of State Legislatures), 33.

Figure 3.5. Source of Taxable Retail Sales, by Retail Type, 2004–05

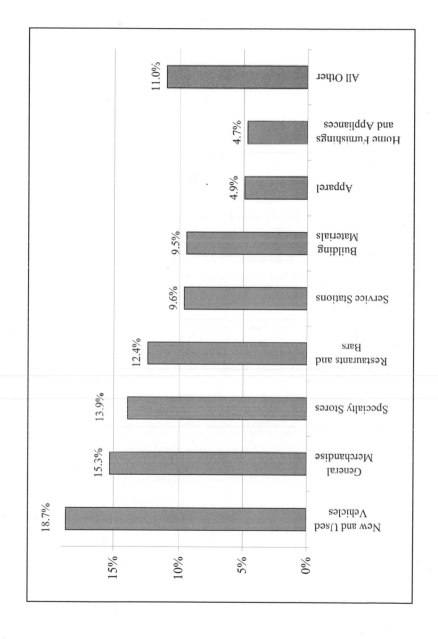

other consumer transactions—could generate an additional $36 billion for the state.[18]

But the sales tax base is not easily or often changed. In 2008, Governor Schwarzenegger proposed a modest extension to a limited list of services, and his proposal was roundly defeated. In 1991, the last time the Legislature considered a broad expansion, Governor Wilson proposed extending what, essentially, was a sales tax on telecommunications (for an annual revenue gain of $800 million). Assembly Speaker Willie Brown proposed applying the sales tax to entertainment for an annual revenue gain of about $350 million. In the end, the negotiated budget settlement did not include either of these base-broadening measures. Instead, the budget included sales tax expansions for candy and snack food, newspapers, jet fuel, and bottled water for an annual gain of nearly $500 million.

Even after the Legislature's approval of these base broadeners, the 1991 changes remained controversial. When the State Board of Equalization, which regulates and collects the sales tax, attempted to implement the tax on snack foods it had trouble distinguishing between snack and nonsnack foods. While a cookie could easily be considered a "snack," it was less clear whether a granola bar should be considered a "snack" subject to tax. Representatives of grocery chains and bottled water distributors signed the ballot argument for the repeal of the tax. They implied in the 1992 *Voters Pamphlet*[19] that the tax expansion could lead to taxing the life's "essentials," such as food, saying,

> We have a proud tradition in California of not taxing the essentials of life. . . .
> A sales tax is the most regressive levy that places the greatest tax burden on
> those who can least afford the tax. And an even worse policy is to place a sales
> tax on food. This is the first step toward a tax on all food products in California.

On November 3, 1992, the voters approved a proposition repealing the 1991 "snack tax."

Given the difficulty of broadening it, the sales tax base remains much as it was during the twentieth century, and is applied to most retail transactions of "tangible personal property." The notable tax expenditures are the sales of food for home preparation, utilities, and prescription medicines. About 90 percent of the value of the tax expenditures derived from exemptions extended to the purchase of food and utilities. The food exemption attempts to distinguish between food necessary for sustaining life and luxuries. Thus, the exemption applies to the purchase of food for home consumption (like fruits and vegetables) and food purchased for preparation at home (like cake mixes, and raw meat, and fish). Certain production inputs, like fertilizer for crops and feed for cattle, are exempt. But there is no exemption for prepared foods served at restaurants or bought from grocery stores. As a result, the raw chicken bought at

---

[18] Bill Lockyer, *Looking beyond the Horizon: Investment Planning for the 21st Century* (Sacramento, Calif., 2007), 33.
[19] *California Voters Pamphlet*, November 3, 1992, 41.

Safeway's meat department is exempt, but the roasted chicken bought in the same store's delicatessen section is taxed. The food exemption reduces taxes by $4.0 billion (46.0 percent of the total exemptions).[20]

The other large exemption class, the utilities exemption, reduces taxes on the sale or transfer of piped potable water, gas, and most forms of electricity and heat production.

The utilities exemption reduces state revenues by $2.2 billion (24.9 percent of the total exemptions). The exemption is generally justified as a way of reducing the tax on "necessities," though the exemption applies to sales to businesses as well as sales for home consumption. It can also be justified as a way of preventing the state from crowding out a local tax base, as many cities and counties apply a utility user tax to the sale of electricity and gas. The local tax generates revenues in excess of $1.5 billion annually.

The purchase of all prescription medicines—considered another "necessity" —are exempt from the sales tax, reducing revenues by about $1.7 billion (representing 19.5 percent of the value of the sales tax exemptions). The purchase of candy, snack foods, and bottled water reduced tax revenues by $382 million. All other exemptions reduce taxes by less than $500 million. Figure 3.6 displays the relative value of these tax expenditures.[21]

The Other Revenue Sources

In 2007–08, revenue derived from the Corporation Tax accounted for $10.7 billion, about 8.5 percent of total state revenues. Motor vehicle fuel taxes are per-gallon levies on the sale of gasoline, diesel, and alternative fuels (including liquefied petroleum gas, liquid natural gas, compressed natural gas, and alcohol fuel). The rates are set in the California Constitution at 18 cents per gallon, and the tax generated about $3.5 billion. Other major taxes include:

- The insurance tax, which generates $2.2 billion annually, and is levied on the value of the premiums written. Nearly half the tax is paid on life and disability plans. The tax rate, 2.35 percent for most plans, is set in the constitution.
- The motor vehicle registration and weight fees, which are set in statute, are levied on all vehicles annually. The fees vary by type of vehicle and generate about $2.8 billion annually.
- The cigarette tax, which generates $1.0 billion each year. Proposition 10, adopted by the voters in 1998, increased the excise tax imposed on distribu-

[20] Department of Finance "Schedule 8," *Governor's Budget Summary 2009* (Sacramento: Calif.).

[21] Department of Finance, "Table 3," *Tax Expenditure Report 2008–09* (Sacramento, Calif.).

Figure 3.6. Share of Sales Tax Exemptions, by Major Category, 2006–07

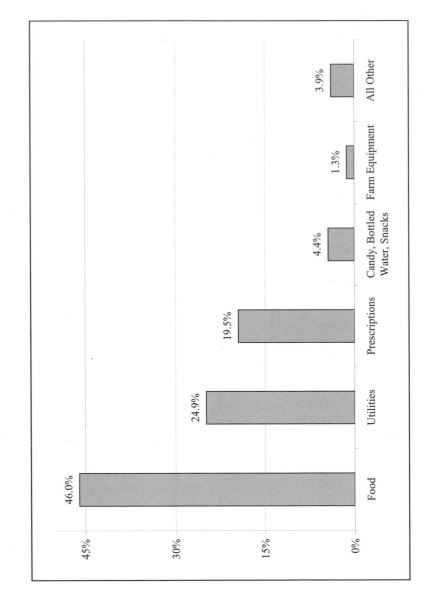

tors selling cigarettes in California to 87 cents per pack, with most of the new revenue earmarked for health programs.

• The alcoholic beverage tax, which generates about $327.3 million annually and is levied on the sale of beer, wine, and distilled spirits. Statute sets the rates, which are levied on the volume of the beverage and vary by type of beverage.

Taken together and as displayed in Table 3.2, the major taxes—predominately the income and sales taxes—produced $111.8 billion (about 85.7 percent of all revenue) in 2007–08.

For the other revenue sources, the single largest category, "regulatory" taxes and fees, generated about $5.7 billion, most of which were deposited in over 30 special funds. The two largest individual revenue sources were the beverage container recycling charge (which generated about $1.1 billion) and the energy resources surcharge (which generated about $633 million.) The Legislature authorized the surcharge, but the California Energy Commission sets the rate annually. The tax is imposed on utility bills. Regulatory taxes and fees accounted for about 4.4 percent of all state revenues in 2007–08.

The state sold a medium-term "deficit bond" and deposited the proceeds in the General Fund, to generate $3.3 billion in revenue, about 2.5 percent of all revenue in 2007–08.

The state also generates revenue from the use or sale of assets, including idle cash. In 2007–08, the state generated about $1.5 billion in revenue from its activities, representing 1.2 percent of all revenue. Interest earned on surplus and pooled cash generated about $900 million of this amount.

The other categories of revenues generated 5.5 percent of all revenues.

The Importance of the General Fund

General Fund revenues, which accounted for $105.9 billion (about 81.1 percent of all revenues) in 2007–08, are distinguished from other revenues because they are levied on a wide cross-section of taxpayers and collected without statutory or constitutional limits on their public use. The Legislature has broad discretion to allocate the revenues to any state purpose. The Legislature makes tax policy without calibrating whether a taxpayer will benefit in proportion to the amount of taxes she pays. Decisions about tax rates and bases are made reflecting other policy considerations, such as the state's ability to collect and the ease of administering the tax. By separating the decision about what is taxed from the decision about the allocation of the proceeds from general taxes, the Legislature affords itself more flexibility about how it imposes General Fund taxes.

Because of their volume and the Legislature's broad discretion when levying the taxes and using their proceeds, General Fund revenues command the greatest legislative attention during budget negotiations. As displayed in Table 3.2, two taxes—income and sales taxes—generate the greatest amount of General Fund

Table 3.2. Revenues and Transfers, 2007–08 (Dollars in Millions)

	General Fund	Special Fund	Total Amount Amount	Total Amount Percent
Major Taxes				
Personal Income Tax	$ 54,234.0	$ 1,512.0	$ 55,746.0	
Sales Tax	26,613.2	5,359.6	31,972.8	
All Other Major Taxes	14,495.4	9,567.0	24,062.4	
Subtotal, Major Taxes	$ 95,342.6	$ 16,438.6	$111,781.2	85.7%
Regulatory Revenues	551.7	5,137.6	5,689.3	4.4%
Bond Proceeds	3,313.0		3,313.0	2.5%
Use of Property	907.8	640.5	1,548.3	1.2%
Revenues from Locals	261.1	833.9	1,095.0	0.8%
Services to Public	45.1	417.9	463.0	0.4%
Loans and Transfers	1,236.8	-613.4	623.4	0.5%
Miscellaneous	4,229.0	1,765.1	5,994.1	4.6%
Totals	$ 105,887.1	$ 24,620.2	$130,507.3	
Percent of Total	81.1%	18.9%		

revenues. Proceeds from the personal income tax accounted for half the of all General Fund revenue in 2007–08.[22] Please see Figure 3.7.

Revenues deposited in the other funds, known collectively as "special funds" to distinguish them from the General Fund, are earmarked for specific programs, and total over $25 billion (about 20 percent of total state revenues). The disposition of the revenues is displayed in Table 3.2, by major revenue source.

Special fund revenues may be derived from taxes or fees. Special fund taxes often share the same tax base as General Fund revenues. The law earmarks a portion of the sales, income, cigarette, and alcohol taxes into special funds. For example, about 10 percent of the revenue derived from the cigarette tax is deposited in the General Fund. The balance, almost $1 billion, is distributed to three different special funds. Most of the earmarks were made by statewide initiatives to raise the tax rate and allocate the new revenue to the Children and Families First Trust and the Cigarette and Tobacco Products Surtax Funds. The initiatives did not differentiate between the special or general tax base. Table 3.3 displays the allocation of cigarette tax revenue by fund. In the case of other taxes, when the proceeds of an entire tax—like the proceeds of the excise tax on gasoline—are earmarked, all the revenue derived form the tax are deposited in a special fund. Special funds may also derive revenues from fees directly imposed for a service provided. The charge may be set in statute or the Legislature may delegate the rate-setting to the collecting body. The law distinguishes fees from taxes. Fees have a direct link between the amount paid by the fee payer and the services provided. The Legislature can levy fees with a majority vote while the state constitution requires that tax increases be approved with a two-thirds vote of each house. The fees may not exceed the cost of the service provided. Inherent in the levying of fees for service is a dedication to the limited purposes for which the fee is collected. For example, university fees must be used to support student activities in the California State University system, and cannot be reallocated to support the Department of Motor Vehicles.

Shaping Tax Policy, One Year at a Time

From 1991 to 2007, the governor and Legislature collaborated on reshaping the state's tax policy. After raising taxes by billions of dollars in 1991 with bipartisan votes, they then reduced taxes—on a broad, bipartisan basis—in nearly every subsequent year, while managing state fiscal affairs in the face of wild fluctuations in the state's financial fortunes.

---

[22] Department of Finance, "Schedule 8," *Governor's Budget Summary 2009* (Sacrament, Calif.).

Figure 3.7. Major Sources of Components of General Fund Revenue, 2007–08 (Dollars in Millions)

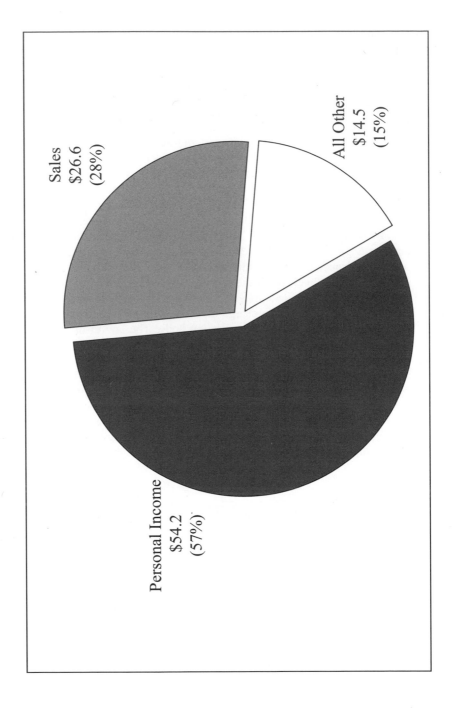

Sales
$26.6
(28%)

All Other
$14.5
(15%)

Personal Income
$54.2
(57%)

Table 3.3. Levies and Revenues on Tobacco Products, 2008–09 (Dollars in Millions)

	Tax Per Pack	Revenue
California Children and Families First Trust Fund	0.50	$ 616.0
Cigarette and Tobacco Products Surtax Fund	0.25	335.0
General Fund	0.10	119.4
Breast Cancer Fund	0.02	24.0
Total	0.87	$ 1,094.4

In light of the current and dramatic problems that seem to defy resolution it is received wisdom to blame the state's political leadership—Democratic and Republican legislators and three governors—for failing to be prudent stewards of the state's fiscal affairs. A more careful reading of the state's recent fiscal management shows, instead, that the state's leadership—on a bipartisan and continuing basis—took extraordinary care to try to manage the state's long-term fiscal condition. Throughout the period, they endeavored to reduce taxes without compromising essential services. Though their efforts, in the end, did not sufficiently protect the state from the effects of unanticipated revenue reductions, the state's deficits derived from something other than the failure of fiscal controls.

Tax changes do not happen in a vacuum. With economic and fiscal conditions helping to shape tax policy, the history of the tax changes can be grouped into three phases, reflecting the state's larger economic and fiscal trends. In 1991, the Legislature raised revenues by increasing all the state's major taxes, including raising tax rates on the income, corporation, and sales taxes. The Legislature took few tax actions in 1992 and 1993. Beginning in 1994, though, as the state enjoyed an expanding economy and an unprecedented increase in income tax revenues, legislators initiated the second phase, in which they reduced taxes. Most memorably, they reduced the state's tax on vehicles. Income and corporation taxes were reduced as well. In the final phase starting in 2002, when the revenue surge faltered, the Legislature again raised taxes. When all the tax increases and tax cuts are netted out, Californians were paying about the same amount in taxes in 2005 as they were in 1990.

During these years, the Legislature and governor collaborated to change who paid the state's taxes. They also worked together to find inventive and responsible ways to provide tax relief.

The tax changes were typically made in legislation implementing a budget compromise. While the legislative process tends to separate budget and tax legislation, the connection between the budget and tax policy is sometimes explicit, as it was in January 2000 when Governor Davis proposed exempting teachers' salaries from the personal income tax. By eliminating the tax on teachers' salaries, he hoped to increase teachers' take-home pay without having to increase the budget for salaries or other compensation.

1991 through 1993: Bipartisan Agreement to Raise Taxes

To help balance the budget in 1991, the Legislature approved an increase in General Fund and special fund taxes. Though the tax increase was *estimated* to raise revenues by $7.3 billion,[23] *actual* revenues increased by only about $6.1 billion. The difference from the estimate was the result of continued economic contraction in 1991 and 1992.

To raise over $6 billion in 1991, the Legislature increased all the major taxes, including the income, sales, corporations, alcoholic beverage, and vehicle license taxes. (Though the state constitution earmarks the proceeds of the vehicle license tax to cities and counties, state statute at the time controlled the tax base and rate. Legislators used the increased vehicle revenue to pay for programs that were shifted to local governments.) Most of the higher revenue, about $5.4 billion (nearly 90 percent), was attributable to rate increases in the income, sales, and alcoholic beverage taxes. The Legislature imposed two new top tax rates on high-income taxpayers, raised the sales tax rate from 4.75 percent to 5.50 percent, and increased the alcohol tax rate to generate about 150 percent more revenue. It increased vehicle license tax revenues by an average of about 20 percent. The Legislature also eliminated tax exemptions in the sales, income, and corporation taxes. The Legislature extended the sales tax to the purchase of candy, snack food, and bottled water for an annualized tax increase of about $200 million. It imposed the sales tax on newspapers and periodicals for an $80 million tax increase, and required trucks, ships, and airplanes to pay sales tax on the fuel bought in California for consumption out of state for a $100 million tax increase. The Legislature conformed to federal tax law, which increased annual revenues by about $300 million.

The governor and Legislature were concerned about tax burdens, so they did not make all the tax increases permanent. Some tax increases expired on specific dates. The half-cent sales tax increase was subject to statutory repeal on July 1, 1993. The top income tax rates would apply only to the tax years 1991 through 1995. When the Legislature suspended a corporation's ability to claim net operating losses for two years, it raised taxes by about $900 million over the two years. (The restored credit allowed corporations to claim a greater percentage of their subsequent losses, thereby reducing corporate taxes beginning in 1993.) When the Legislature delayed for one year the implementation of the corporate tax credit for small employers providing health care to employees, it only raised taxes for a year.

Other tax increases were subject to repeal when specific fiscal conditions were met. One condition provided for an automatic tax repeal if counties prevailed in a court case against the state. Prior to the 1991 budget, the state, and counties shared fiscal and administrative responsibility for mental health, indigent care, and local health services. As part of the 1991 budget, the state reduced its financial

---

[23] Legislative Analyst's Office, *State Spending Plan for 1991–92* (Sacramento, Calif.: Legislative Analyst's Office, 1991), 51 and 53.

commitment to these programs, shifting the administrative and fiscal responsibilities to the counties. At the time the Legislature debated the transaction, known as "realignment," the Department of Finance raised concerns about pending lawsuits that could increase the state's costs for funding state mandates to pay for county health programs. Thomas Hayes, the director of finance and former state treasurer and state auditor, knew that these lawsuits, if decided against the state, could require the state to fund not only the "realigned" programs but also previous transactions that had shifted costs from the state to local governments. In the event the state lost its court cases, it might want to use the realignment revenues to pay for the previously mandated local expenditures rather than the new realignment program. To protect the state's future fiscal flexibility, the laws raising the realignment revenue contained provisions to repeal the realignment transaction if the counties won their mandate lawsuits. These provisions were referred to as "poison pills" because they ensured that the state would repeal (that is, "kill") the realignment proposal whenever counties succeeded in their lawsuit.

Another condition provided for reducing the sales tax by a quarter-cent if the state ran a four percent end-of-year surplus. This provision was adopted to address Republican concerns about what GOP legislators perceived as excessive tax increases. The quarter-cent increase was the last tax increase proposed as part of the 1991 budget. The budget conference committee proposed it in June, after the Legislature and governor had negotiated in earnest for over five months about how to finance the deficit. In June, it became clear that the gap had grown again (after reviewing the mid-year tax receipts), and that there was no enthusiasm for more cuts to close the gap. When this last tax was proposed in the conference committee, the Senate Republican conferee, Frank Hill, acknowledged that some people thought there were no additional spending cuts available so additional taxes were necessary. However, he found it unlikely that he could convince the Senate Republican caucus to agree to yet another tax increase. To address his concerns, he suggested that the last tax increase be repealed whenever the state returned to fiscal health. He suggested that the measure of fiscal health be whenever the state's end-of-year reserve reached four percent two years in a row.

Governor Wilson expected that the state's revised tax base would fully finance the state's ongoing program costs for the rest of his term. By raising taxes to balance estimated revenues with estimated expenditures, he hoped to shift his administration's focus from the budget deficit to policy initiatives beginning in 1992. Instead, as the state's recession continued—and despite the 1991 tax increases—the state faced a budget deficit of $11.2 billion. The 1991 tax increases were not enough to balance the 1992 budget, and he found himself in budget negotiations through September 1992. Neither he nor the Legislature relished raising taxes again. They approved but one tax hike in 1992.[24] By again delaying

---

[24] In this year, the Legislature also deferred refunding to the federal government sales tax inappropriately levied on federal contractors. The tax refund, required pursuant to a court decision, had the state pay the federal government nearly $600 million for sales

implementation of the small-employer health credit, the Legislature increased budget-year revenues by $100 million.[25]

In 1993–94, the state continued to face a large budget deficit. In May, the legislative analyst, the Legislature's nonpartisan budget office, identified a budget-year deficit of about $5.7 billion. The deficit was due in part to the scheduled statutory repeal of the half-cent sales tax. When the Legislature raised the sales tax rate in 1991, it provided for a statutory sunset on July 1, 1993, with the effect of reducing revenues by nearly $1.5 billion annually starting in 1993–94. The voters also reduced revenues by about $300 million when they approved Proposition 163, repealing the sales tax on candy, snack foods, and bottled water. To help address the gap, the Legislature took four actions to raise revenues. First, it permanently repealed the small employer health credit, which it had been delaying for the last two years, to raise taxes by $100 million annually. Second, it suspended the income tax credit for renters, increasing revenues by about $400 million. Then, the Legislature extended for six months the half-cent sales tax increase, which had been scheduled to expire on July 1, 1994. The extension yielded a revenue gain of about $700 million. Fourth, legislators authorized a special election in November 1993 for the purpose of seeking the electorate's approval of a permanent extension of the half-cent sales tax. The ballot measure earmarked the proceeds of the tax to local law enforcement and raised nearly $1.5 billion annually. The voters approved the legislative initiative, which was placed on the ballot as Proposition 172.

Between 1991 and 1993, the Legislature struggled to balance a budget that seemed to run chronic, large deficits. Over the three years, taxpayers paid $17 billion more in taxes than they would have had no tax change occurred. Table 3.4 cumulates the tax changes for the three years ending June 30, 1994, and shows the effect by fiscal year. The largest revenue gains derived from increased rates on the sales tax. The legislatively levied sales tax increases generated $9.5 billion in new taxes and the voter-approved Proposition 172 increased taxes by another $1.4 billion. Higher income tax rates generated $2.7 billion in new revenue. Vehicle owners paid $1.5 billion more in license fees. See Table 3.4 for details.

Nearly two-thirds of the new revenue came from the sales tax. This heavy reliance on the sales tax is troubling to those who believe that the sales tax imposes a disproportionate burden on low-income Californians. Nevertheless, it appears that Californians supported the imposition of the sales tax, as they approved the sales tax levy proposed on the November statewide ballot. The impact of this "tax on the poor" was somewhat balanced by the personal income tax rate increases. The income tax rate increases accounted for about 15 percent of the total increase. Taken together, the changes in the sales and income taxes were 80 percent of the total tax change.

---

taxes collected in prior years. The refund did not raise tax levels on consumers, contractors, or the federal government.

[25] Legislative Analyst's Office, *State Spending Plan for 1992–93* (Sacramento, Calif.: Legislative Analyst's Office, 1992), 8.

Table 3.4. 1991–92 through 1993–94, (Dollars in Millions)

	1991–92	1992–93	1993–94
Legislatively Approved			
1991–92			
Increase Alcohol Tax Rates	$ 203	$ 184	$ 181
Add Top Income Tax Rate	1,060	849	750
Increase Sales Tax Base	400	120	126
Sales Tax Rate	2,440	2,264	770
Sales Tax Rate (Local)	1,258	1,378	1,426
Net Operating Loss	257	401	-377
Vehicle License	473	486	493
Suspend Health Care Credit	100		
1992–93			
Repeal Health Care Credit		100	103
1993–94			
Suspend Renters Credit			390
Subtotal, Legislatively Approved	$ 6,191	$ 5,782	$ 3,862
Voter Approved			
Proposition 172			1,387
Totals	$6,191	$5,782	$ 5,249

The governor and Legislature tried to mitigate the long-term impact of the tax changes by making many of them temporary. Or, as in the case of the final quarter-cent sales tax rate increase, they provided for an automatic statutory reduction whenever the state's fiscal condition improved. Though the state increased taxes by $6.2 billion in 1991, the taxes adopted during the first three Wilson years were only generating $5.2 billion in 1996.

The state's political leadership tried to secure fiscal reforms, too, as they raised taxes. This was explicitly so when they negotiated the "realignment" of state and local fiscal responsibilities. Though it raised taxes to pay for more local programs, the Legislature charged the counties with greater responsibility for managing costs of the realigned programs.

Perhaps—at this distance—the most startling aspect of the 1991 tax increases is the bipartisan nature of the votes. To be sure, Democrats proposed broader and higher tax increases, but the Republican governor and legislative leadership supported major tax changes. The affirmative votes on the tax measures often carried more than the minimum number of Republicans required for passage.

1994 to 2002: Taxes Reduced

The 1991 tax increases—dramatic and broad—cast a long shadow for the next decade. Though two-thirds of each house voted for the tax increases, Democratic and Republican members alike heard the complaints at home. Reacting to those objections, Governor Wilson and legislative leaders pledged to impose no new taxes because Californians were, in Wilson's words, "taxed to the max."[26] Keeping this pledge, though, did not prevent Wilson (or his successor Gray Davis) and subsequent legislatures from making adjustments in the tax structure to change who paid the taxes. In each year between 1994 and 2001, the Legislature changed which Californians paid taxes and how much they paid. Indeed, by 1994, both the governor and Legislature were prepared to cut taxes, even as they grappled with a $2 billion deficit.

Some of this deficit was attributable to the expiration of the increased income tax rates adopted for the highest earners. Collections for withholding for the remaining top rates fell by about $325 million[27] in 1994–95. Though the Legislature suspended the renters credit again to raise taxes by $400 million, it also enacted a major new tax relief program for corporations. By authorizing a tax credit for six percent of the cost of manufacturing equipment, it intended to provide incentives for manufacturers locating or upgrading their equipment in California. The credit reduced taxes by $80 million in 1994, and when fully implemented, the credit reduced revenues by $400 million annually. To overcome this opposition, the credit's sponsors agreed to a set of statutory conditions repealing the credit. Rather than specify a year (e.g., 2001) in which the credit would sunset, the supporters proposed an automatic repeal in whatever year the Employment Development Department determined that the number of California's manufacturing jobs fell below a target amount.

In 1995, the state faced a small deficit. To close this budget gap, the Legislature suspended the renters credit again to raise taxes by about $400 million. Later in that year, the state began recovering from the recession and benefited from an unprecedented change in taxable investment income. Beginning in 1995, income tax revenue grew from $20 billion to $44.6 billion, a 17 percent average annual growth rate. In each year beginning in 1996, the Legislature used part of these revenue gains and surpluses to finance tax reductions, intending to offset the revenue increases from the previous five years. In 1996, the Legislature reduced corporate tax rates by five percent and adopted a phased-in package of business

---

[26] *Los Angeles Times*, January 7, 1992.
[27] Legislative Analyst's Office, *State Spending Plan for 1994–95* (Sacramento, Calif.: Legislative Analyst's Office), 56.

tax incentives, reducing corporate taxes by about $110 million. It also adopted legislation to conform state law to federal tax changes, raising individual taxes by about $25 million. It suspended the renters credit again, for a one-year revenue gain of $400 million. Although the 1996 package raised taxes by a net amount of about $300 million for 1996–97, the out-year effect of the changes was to reduce tax loads. The corporate tax rate change was phased in so that, when fully implemented, the package reduced taxes on a net annual basis by about $350 million.

On January 10, 1997, Governor Wilson proposed a budget that assumed a phased-in 10 percent reduction in the bank and corporation tax rate. This reduction, when combined with the 1996 cut, was intended to reduce corporate taxes by about $600 million when fully phased-in by 2000–01. Later in the year, the governor also proposed a 10 percent reduction for personal income tax rates. The Democratic majority in the Legislature rejected both of these proposals and directed its leadership to negotiate an alternative tax relief package to be implemented over a three-year phase-in period. The negotiation continued throughout the summer, well after the budget had been signed.

By the end of August, Wilson and the Legislature agreed to a package. The most expensive change was to increase the dependent credit in the income tax. They agreed to phase in an increase for the per-dependent credit amount from $68 to $120 in 1998, and $222 in subsequent years. The higher credit reduced income taxes for nearly three million taxpayers by about $300 million in 1998–99 and $760 million the following year.

Also in the package, the governor and legislators agreed to simplify tax filing by changing the requirement that taxpayers with middle-class incomes calculate the alternative minimum tax. Middle-income taxpayers were relieved from both the headache of making the minimum tax calculation and the risk of having to pay additional tax. The provision reduced taxes by $44 million in its first year.

In another tax-simplifying move, the Legislature conformed state tax law to recent federal tax law changes. These changes reduced taxes by about $100 million in the first year and about $200 million when fully implemented. The largest conformity item, worth about $60 million annually, allows corporations to deduct research and development costs

The tax relief was offset by another one-year suspension of the renters credit. On a net basis, the 1997 package raised taxes by about $200 million in 1997–98 but when the higher dependent credit amount was fully phased-in, the package lowered taxes by over $1 billion.

In 1998, the Legislature extended tax relief for the third year in a row. It raised the value of the dependent credit again, this time from $120 to $253—but only for the 1998 tax year, with the effect of reducing taxes on a one-time basis by $600 million. It provided tax relief to senior citizens and the disabled by expanding the eligibility for the Senior Citizens Tax Relief Program. The program reimburses seniors and disabled persons for a portion of the property tax paid on their residence (irrespective of whether the person owns or rents the property). The reimbursement amount is inversely related to income so that higher-income taxpayers receive a lower reimbursement. The program limits participation to taxpayers with incomes below a statutory threshold, beginning in 1999. In 1998, the Legislature increased the threshold from $13,200 to $33,000 so that more taxpayers qualified for relief. By raising and indexing the income qualification threshold, the change provided tax relief worth about $70 million annually.

Most significantly in 1998—not coincidently in Wilson's last year as governor—the governor and Legislature experimented with innovative ways to make tax policy. The Legislature would continue these experiments with the next governor. In one 1998 experiment, they conditioned the implementation of a package of targeted tax reductions upon the electoral fate of a statewide initiative, Proposition 7. The proposition, which was on the November 1998 statewide ballot, would have authorized the annual allocation of up to $218 million in tax credits for improving air quality. The Legislature authorized a substitute set of targeted tax credits if the proposition failed. The reductions were phased in from a value of about $50 million in 1998–99 to $100 million by 2002–03. Throughout the next five years, the Legislature would try other ways of using statutory devices—variations on the poison pill—to place conditions on tax cuts.

The Legislature also began its long experiment in reducing the vehicle license fee. At the time, the vehicle license fee represented about nine percent of the state's total tax revenue stream. The Legislature focused on the vehicle license fee in part as a reaction to political events on the East Coast. During Virginia's 1997 gubernatorial race, the Republican nominee, James S. Gilmore III, campaigned hard to repeal the property tax on vehicles for personal use. The average tax rate was about four percent. On the stump, Gilmore despaired over how the "car tax"—as he described it—was administered. Each of the state's 135 cities and counties had discretion about how they applied the tax. Some assessed vehicles based on their trade-in value. Others used the value of the car's loan, retail price, wholesale price, or blue book entry. Based on the success of his "cut the car-tax" campaign, Gilmore won with a 13-point advantage over the Democrat, Donald S. Beyer, Jr. On his inaugural day in 1998, Governor Gilmore proposed legislation to cut the tax by reducing the vehicle's assessed value by 70 percent. The tax reduction was phased in over five years, and it was conditioned on Virginia's fiscal condition.[28] The tax relief would be provided only if Virginia continued to run budget surpluses. Commercial trucks, panel trucks, motor homes, farm vehicles, and trailers did not qualify for the reduction.

California adopted some aspects of the Virginia law. Like the Virginia governor, the California Legislature wanted to phase in the relief in future years. Sensitive to its limitations in predicting future budget circumstances, the Legislature provided for phased in future reductions only if state revenues were sufficient to support government expenditures. California, however, started from a different place than Virginia. Unlike Virginia, California's existing method of taxation was uniform. Its tax rate was two percent, half the rate in Virginia. Unlike

---

[28] Mike Allen, "Legislature to Focus on Tax Cut," *Washington Post,* January 11, 1998, B1.

Virginia, California did not limit the tax relief to passenger cars and trucks. The California tax reduction applied to all vehicles, including commercial vehicles and motor homes. It reduced the vehicle license fee by 25 percent in 1998, cutting taxes by $533 million in 1998–99.

The Legislature again offset a part of the tax reductions with an increase in the renter's credit. In this year, however, rather than suspend the credit, the Legislature made a permanent change to the credit. Prior to the change, the tax code authorized a $60 refundable credit for each renter. With the 1998 change, the Legislature made the credit nonrefundable. As a nonrefundable credit, renters could still claim a credit against their income taxes of up to $60 per year. If, after computing her taxes, a renter determined that she owed $100 in taxes, she could claim the full $60 credit. However, if she owed $50, she could claim a renter's credit of $50. By making the credit nonrefundable, the Legislature cut the cost of the credit by about three-quarters, raising annual taxes by about $300 million.

In total, the tax changes cost the state a net amount of about $1.3 billion in the first year and $1.6 billion annually thereafter.

In the 1998 November election, Gray Davis succeeded Pete Wilson. In Davis's first year, 1999, the state ran a budget surplus. Davis and the Legislature used part of the surplus to again reduce the vehicle license fee by $500 million— for one year only. The Legislature also conformed state law to federal income tax laws allowing the self-employed to deduct their health insurance costs (reducing state revenue by $21 million in 1999–2000, with a full-implementation annual cost of over $80 million). It reduced the tax on capital gains on small business stock (costing $3 million in 1999–00, rising to $44 million in future years). It increased the research and development credit for an annual cost of less than $10 million. In all, the 1999 tax changes cost about $140 million in 1999–00 and $400 million annually thereafter.

In 2000, with the state again running a large budget surplus, the Legislature adopted an income tax credit for credentialed teachers. The law limited the value of the credit to half the individual's teaching income, and reduced taxes by about $200 million annually. The Legislature also adopted a refundable credit for child care expenses modeled on federal tax law. The amount of the credit is inversely related to income. For those earning $40,000 or less, the state credit is 63 percent of the federal credit amount and varies in income. For those earning between $40,000 and $70,000 the credit is 53 percent of the federal amount. For those earning between $70,000 and $100,000, it is 42 percent. Those making in excess of $100,000 do not qualify for the credit. The program reduced revenues by about $200 million a year.

For the third year in a row, the Legislature experimented with providing tax relief for vehicle owners, and passed legislation to both increase the amount of relief and accelerate the phase in of the amount of the vehicle fee reduction it had authorized in 1998. Under the change, the phase in would be completed in 2001 rather than 2003. By accelerating the tax relief, the provision cost the state about $1 billion in 2000–01, $1.5 billion in 2001–02, $800 million in 2002–03 and $700 million in 2003–04.

In the spirit of innovation, the Legislature approved an "appropriated" tax credit. The tax credit was for the value of land donated for the public use. The statutory law charged the administration with allocating the credit. The annual amount of the credit was to be set in the annual budget act.

There were two temporary tax changes. For the 2000 tax year only, legislators increased by 150 percent the value of the senior citizens property tax assistance program, providing $154 million in increased tax relief. For the tax years 2000 through 2004, legislators authorized a credit to qualified taxpayers providing health care to individuals. Under the change, a taxpayer could claim a $500 credit for each individual receiving care, provided that the claimant had a taxable income of less than $100,000. The Legislature expected the credit to cost about $40 million.

In November 2000, Tim Gage, the director of the Department of Finance, determined that the state had run large General Fund surpluses. In making the determination, he invoked the conditions of the 1991 quarter-cent trigger. The trigger adopted as part of that year's tax increases provided that the sales tax rate would fall in any year following two years of surpluses. When Gage issued this determination, state taxes were reduced by about $600 million for the 2001–02 year.

Ironically, the trigger was activated in the last year of budget surpluses, well after the state had "recovered" from the recession sustained in the early 1990s. In 2001, with a softening economy and falling income tax revenues, Gage believed that was not the year to reduce sales tax revenues. To protect the General Fund, he negotiated with the Republicans a revision to the trigger, making it more likely that the state raised the sales tax under deficit circumstances.

In addition to the triggered sales tax reduction, the Legislature and governor provided for a permanent 45 percent increase in the senior citizens property tax assistance program, additional tax relief of $75 million. Agricultural businesses and rural residents received targeted tax reductions worth about $50 million annually.

During this second phase, extraordinary investment-income gains in the late 1990s allowed the Legislature to cut taxes significantly. Overall, the Legislature reduced taxes by about $16 billion for the eight-year period beginning in 1994–95. Of this, $8 billion was provided through the reduction in the car tax. Another $4 billion in tax relief was extended to corporations through a corporate tax rate reduction and the Manufacturer's Investment Credit. Families with dependents received tax relief of nearly $3 billion. Renters, however, paid about $3 billion more in taxes after they lost the Renters Credit.

The reductions helped to offset the on-going effects of the tax increases imposed in the early 1990s. The legislation authorizes the tax cuts, like the earlier legislation to raise taxes, was passed with bipartisan support. In the case of the tax reductions, there was overwhelming legislative support.

While extending these reductions, the Legislature and governor experimented with statutory provisions that could reverse the tax cuts if the state began to evidence fiscal problems. By tying the level of tax relief to the health of the

General Fund, the Legislature attempted to ensure that the state had sufficient revenue to sustain its spending commitments in the event fiscal conditions changed.

After the Bubble: Tax Increases

Between 1996 and 2000, the state experienced dramatic increases in income tax revenue. During these years, income tax revenues grew at 17.8 percent per year—nearly 2.5 times the average annual growth rate for the period from 1991–92 to 2007–08. Figure 3.8 compares actual income tax receipts with a trend line running from 1991–92 to 2007–08. As displayed in the figure, income tax revenues were $44.6 billion in 2000–01, but fell by $11.6 billion the following year. They fell again in 2002–03. Though revenues began to grow again in 2003–04, they did not exceed their 2000–01 level until 2005–06, like a five-year revenue drought. Revenues rose by $18.5 billion between 2002–03 and 2005–06. This figure shows the state experienced dramatic swings in its single largest revenue source for the period beginning in 1998–99.

Much of this revenue variation can be explained by changes in taxpayer investment income. Taxpayers reported $47.5 billion in capital gains for the 1997 tax year, but $118.0 billion three years later. For the 2001 tax year, they reported $49.1 billion. When investment returns collapsed after 2000, income tax revenues fell beginning with the 2001 tax returns. As displayed in Figure 3.9, though the 2001 amount was below—often well below—the amounts reported in 1998, 1999 and 2000.[29]

After the investment bubble burst, income tax revenues returned to levels consistent with the long-term trend identified in Figure 3.8.

The taxes on these income gains also varied over the period. Indeed, by 2004 income tax revenues still had only grown to 80 percent of 2001 levels. Though revenues grew at a moderate rate and consistent with economic growth during the period July 1, 2002 through June 30, 2004, the growth rates for revenues could not match those sustained during the bubble. Figure 3.10 displays taxes (assuming a nine percent rate) on reported capital gains and stock options for the period 1999 through 2009.[30] As displayed in the figure, revenues attributable to taxes on capital gains grew from about $8.2 billion in 1999 to $11.4 billion to 2008, an average annual growth rate of about 3.0 percent. But the figure documents a great deal of year-to-year variation around the trend line. Without the revenue from the capital gains and stock options, the state faced deep and chronic deficits.

The decline in revenues in the middle of the decade tested how well the Legislature's experiment in limiting the vehicle tax reduction would work. The

---

[29] Franchise Tax Board, *Annual Report 2006* (Sacramento, Calif.), 23.

[30] Department of Finance, "Revenue Estimates," *Governor's Budget Summary 2009* (Sacramento, Calif.).

Figure 3. 8. Actual Income Tax Collections vs. Trend Line, 1991–92 through 2008–09 (Dollars in Millions)

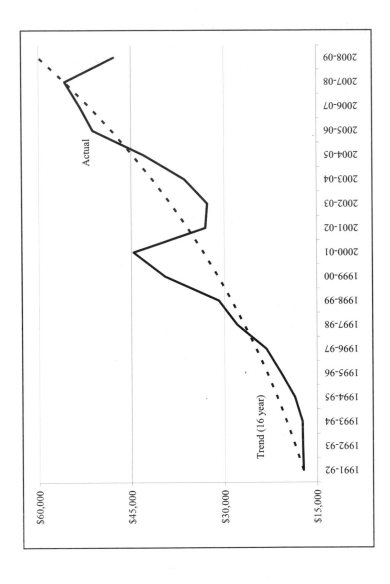

Figure 3.9. Capital Assets Income Taxable Years 1997 through 2005 (Dollars in Billions)

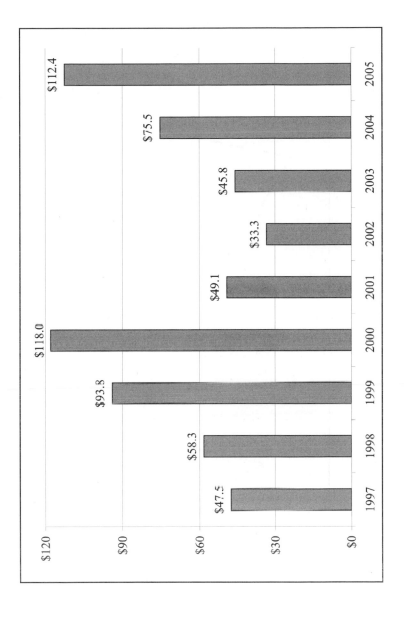

Figure 3.10. Estimated Income Tax on Capital Gains and Stock Options, Assumes 9% Tax Rate (Dollars in Billions)

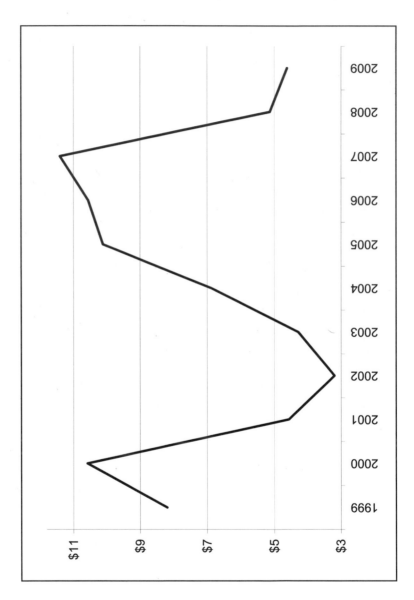

law named *conditions* for automatic repeal of the tax reduction, but it did *not name a party responsible* for making the determination whether the conditions were met. Nor did it name an administrator for ensuring the tax was raised. To use the "trigger" metaphor, though the 1998 law had built a "trigger mechanism," it named no one to "pull the trigger." As a result, the vehicle tax continued at its lower level even as the state began running large deficits. On January 10, 2002, Governor Davis identified a $12 billion deficit.

To close a portion of the deficit, the Legislature approved a tax package to raise taxes by more than $2.2 billion in 2002–03 and $1 billion in 2003–04. The package suspended the credentialed teachers' and natural heritage preservation credits for one year, increasing state revenues by $170 million. The package also conformed state law to federal law in the taxation of bank loan reserves, increasing the tax on banks by about $300 million. Most of the increase—about $1.2 billion—came from a two-year suspension of the tax credit for net operating losses. (Prior to the change, corporations could claim against their tax liability 65 percent of their net operating losses.) The package also provided for ongoing tax reductions beginning in 2004–05. To secure Republican votes for enacting the temporary tax increase, the tax package allowed corporations to claim 100 percent of their losses beginning in 2004–05. This increase in the value of the deduction provided for on-going tax reductions of about $500 million beginning in 2004–05.

At the end of the 2002 legislative session, Senator Steve Peace, a termed-out Democrat, sought to provide statutory clarification of the car-tax trigger. If the statutory language did not name a specific administrator for increasing the tax, then statutory law could be amended to make responsible the governor's director of finance. Three days before the end of the legislative session, Peace amended a bill in the Senate to clarify who could make the determination. Legislative Counsel determined that because the bill merely clarified prior statute—but did not raise taxes—it needed only a majority vote for passage. The Senate passed the bill on a partisan basis to the Assembly. The Assembly did not take up the bill before the end of session, so the measure died.

In December 2002, the Legislative Analyst identified another deficit of about $21 billion. The governor proposed to increase taxes by an ongoing $8 billion. Senator Jim Brulte, the Senate Minority Leader, rejected the tax proposal by saying the state's fiscal problems were the result of inappropriate expansions in programs rather than insufficient revenues. He called for reducing expenditures or deficit financing rather than raising taxes to balance the budget. In the end, the Legislature adopted a much smaller tax increase than the one proposed by the governor.

Governor Davis changed his fiscal staff at the beginning of 2003. Responding to the state's electricity-market problems, he asked Tim Gage, his trusted director of finance, to work on energy policy. Then, he named Steve Peace, who had been termed-out of the Senate, to be the new budget director. Peace once again sought a change in the vehicle tax trigger. If the Legislature would not pass by two-thirds vote a measure to increase the tax directly, he asked it to pass legislation authorizing the finance director to raise the tax.

On February 3, 2003, the Legislature passed the bill clarifying that the director of finance could increase the vehicle license fee to its higher, pre-1998 rate. In March 2003, Peace declared the tax trigger pulled, with the tax increasing later in the year. He estimated that by raising the tax, he would save the state from having to backfill local governments by $2 billion in 2003–04 and even more in each of the coming years.

Before the tax could rise, however, California voters recalled Governor Davis and elected Arnold Schwarzenegger to take his place. Making good on his campaign promise to reverse Peace's action, Governor Schwarzenegger issued an executive order returning the vehicle tax rate to the lower level.

In the next year, 2003–04, the Legislature considered re-enacting the manufacturer's investment credit. The credit had been created in 1994 with a trigger repealing it if the number of manufacturing jobs fell. When the state's Employment Development Department determined that the number of jobs had fallen below the trigger point, the credit was automatically set for repeal. Though the Legislature considered legislation to override the triggered repeal, the legislation failed. The manufacturer's credit was repealed automatically on January 1, 2004. Annual revenues increased by $300 million.

The only major tax legislation adopted in 2003–04 was a measure to reduce the use of tax shelters, which generated about $1.3 billion over two years. For purposes of an analysis of "tax increases," the tax shelter reform is considered not so much a tax increase as much as a measure to improve compliance with existing laws.

Governor Schwarzenegger proposed no new taxes for the 2004–05 budget, though the final budget deal increased taxes by $200 million. The Legislature and governor agreed to suspend for one year the teacher's tax credit and the natural heritage tax credit.

Immediately after the investment bubble burst, the Legislature took actions to raise taxes by a net amount of $1.9 billion between 2002 and 2004. The tax increases enacted in this period, however, were temporary. The legislation adopted after 2002 provided for ongoing tax reductions to businesses.

Cumulative Effect of Tax Changes Enacted Since 1991

In each year between 1991 and 2007, three governors and nine legislatures agreed to make significant changes to the state's tax laws. Over the period, they raised net tax loads by a cumulative amount of $35 billion. If the higher taxes had been spread over the entire period, tax loads would have been raised by about $1.6 billion in each of the 17 years. In practice, taxes were higher during Governor Wilson's term, but fell in each governor's term thereafter.

Figure 3.11 displays the annual net effect of tax changes enacted by the Legislature since January 1, 1991. The dark horizontal line at the origin (marked $0 on the vertical axis) represents what the tax load would have been without any tax changes. As displayed, the Legislature and the governor raised taxes by about

Figure 3.11. Cumulative Effects of Tax Changes since 1991, Changes by Statute, 1991–92 through 2007–08 (Dollars in Billions)

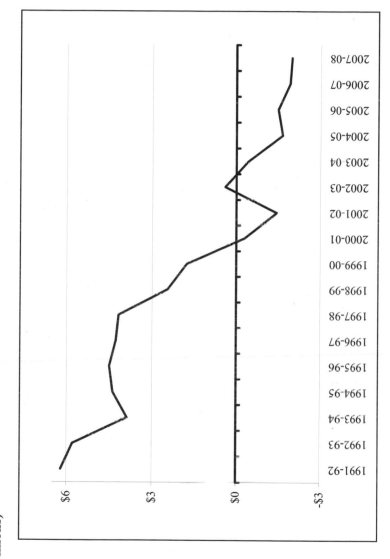

$6 billion in 1991. Then in each year until 2001–02, taxes were reduced relative to this first-year's increase. In 2000–01, tax loads had fallen below what they would have been if the Legislature had taken no action on taxes after January 1, 1991. By 2002–03, tax loads were about $2.5 billion lower. Though the Legislature raised taxes beginning in 2002–03, tax loads only barely rose above the levels required in the 1990 tax law. After that year, the Legislature's actions reduced annual taxes $2.5 billion below what they would have been absent the changes for 2004–05 and forward.

While Figure 3.11 shows that net annual tax loads are lower in 2007 than they were in 1991, it does not display the effect of the changes in the composition of the state's tax systems. Over the period, the Legislature changed *who* paid taxes. Comparing the 1990 tax code to the 2007 code, taxpayers will pay annually about $4 billion more in sales tax because of the sales tax rate increases, while vehicle owners will pay $3 billion less in the vehicle license fee. Families with dependents will pay $1 billion less in income taxes because the state increased the dependent credit.

Figure 3.11 also does not include the effect of Propositions 172 and 63, propositions by which the state's voters raised the sales tax by one-half cent in 1992 and income tax rates in 2004. As displayed in Figure 3.12, after accounting for the tax increases from Propositions 172 and 63, the overall total tax load was slightly higher in 2004 than it would have been if there had been no tax changes from legislation or propositions. Average annual tax burdens are about $3.6 billion higher, or about $61.7 billion more revenue in the 17-year period.

Conclusion

Perhaps the most striking aspect about tax policy after the bubble burst was the failure of the various triggers. The sales tax and car tax triggers were designed to help the state readjust its revenue streams as the state's fiscal condition changed, but they did not provide the kind of self-correcting fiscal response that had been envisioned when they were placed in law. Despite the state leaders' efforts and care in trying to craft a sensitive and realistic tax policy, economic events overwhelmed their ability to manage the state's finances in the short term.

This chapter began with Wilson's observation that voting against taxes was politically expedient. Since then, setting tax policy became increasingly divisive. The change can be seen by contrasting the behavior of Republicans in 1991 and 2002. In 1991, five Republican senators and nine Republican assemblymembers voted for the budget with a tax increase. Newspapers praised Governor Wilson for his leadership. But by 2002, voting "no" had become a matter not of expediency but of survival. On Friday, June 28, 2002, after spending Tuesday and Wednesday

Figure 3.12. Cumulative Effects of Tax Changes Since 1991, Changes by Statute and Propositions 172 and 63, 1991–92 through 2007–08 (Dollars in Billions)

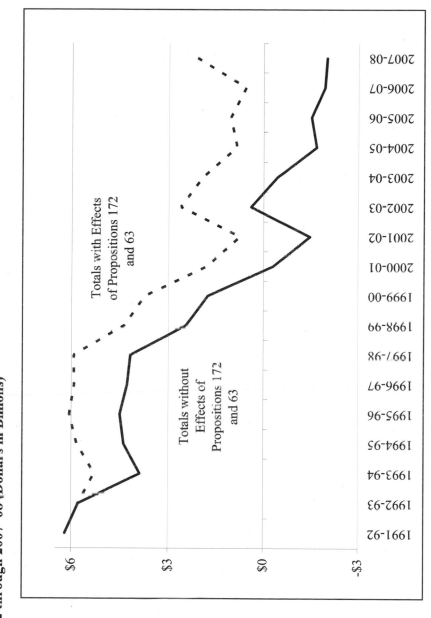

negotiating a budget package with the Democratic leadership, Senator Maurice Johannessen walked on the Senate floor knowing he would be the lone Republican voting for the budget. Though he had successfully negotiated to restore funding on two key Republican concerns—to public safety programs and to counties—he was about to vote for a package that included a $2.3 billion tax increase. His minority colleagues opposed a budget with any tax increase. For some, the effect of the tax increase was not mitigated by the fact that the increase was temporary and fully offset by later, ongoing tax reductions. When he opened his desk on the Senate floor, Johannessen found an anonymous note equating his budget negotiations to the actions of the Scandinavian Nazi collaborator, Vidkun Quisling. In the days following his vote, he was barred altogether from meetings of the Republican caucus. To be sure, over the 14 years between Johannnessen's vote and the earlier Wilson tax increase, voting to raise taxes had become a gut-checking experience exacting a high personal toll.

Chapter 4

Setting Expenditure Policy

For the last 20 years, prominent state politicians fretted about overall spending levels. For example, in a memorandum dated February 15, 1993, Senator Ken Maddy, the Republican Floor Leader, noted that five of the last six budgets ran deficits, saying that the state's continuing fiscal problem was the result of the government's inability to limit expenditures to the amount of annual revenues:

> The root problem is expenditure policy, not a lack of revenues. The state's fiscal history documents that—even before the [1991] recession—the state spent faster than it collected taxes. Given our spending tendencies, it is hard to see how raising taxes resolves our chronic fiscal problems.[1]

This memorandum, delivered at the start of the 1993 budget discussions, was in reaction to the deficits that occurred even after the Legislature raised state taxes by 20 percent in 1991. In distributing his memorandum, Maddy hoped to describe why Republicans would not consider raising taxes to help balance the 1993 budget. Twelve years later, facing another series of chronic deficits, Governor Arnold Schwarzenegger, in his second State of the State speech, echoed Maddy:

---

[1] Kenneth L. Maddy, memorandum to Assembly and Senate Republicans, February 15, 1993.

93

[We] don't have a revenue problem. We have a spending problem. We could raise taxes by billions but that would only further drive up spending by billions of dollars.[2]

These comments—separated by over a decade in which the state experienced unprecedented growth in revenue—reflect a shared premise that deficits result from *unnecessary* spending.

Complaints that the state spends "too much" or "unnecessarily" or "inefficiently" focus budget negotiations on how much spending can be cut without compromising essential services. Too often, this debate affords all participants a great deal of room for rhetorical flourishes but yields very few savings from specific proposals, as happened on December 31, 2008, when the Schwarzenegger administration proposed several measures to close the state's largest-ever deficit. Among its proposals, the administration revived the cuts contained in, but not adopted as part of, its 2004 California Performance Review (CPR). When asked about how much its CPR could save the state relative to the $41 billion deficit, Schwarzenegger's representative said, "It could be upwards of several hundred million [dollars in a single year] as well as billions going out [in cumulative savings over many years]."[3] It seems the savings are as hard to quantify as they are to implement.

Despite the consistent and bipartisan call to "reduce spending," General Fund expenditures rose from $58.8 billion in 1998–99 to $103.6 billion in 2007–08, an average annual increase of about 5.9 percent. At the same time, the state's economy grew at a lower rate. If "reducing spending" is a preferred outcome, both the Legislature and governor can exercise control. The Legislature can refuse to make an appropriation. The governor can use his or her authority to veto spending when signing the budget. Each branch can act decisively and without consulting the other.

State spending patterns are large and diverse enough to defy simple review and explanation. But, how can Californians make sense of this continued rise in spending, in light of the cry for cuts? To provide some context, this chapter considers the following:

(1) The construction of appropriations and how they serve a budget writer's fiscal goals.

(2) How the state spent its General Fund in 2007–08, providing context about relative spending levels.

(3) Changes in spending patterns since 1998.

The chapter focuses on General Fund spending levels, as they get the broadest and most consistent review.

---

[2] Arnold Schwarzenegger, State of the State speech, January 5, 2005.
[3] Steve Wiegand, "'Blow Up the Boxes' Is Back," *The Sacramento Bee*, January 2, 2009, A14.

What Appropriations Reveal about Fiscal Goals

The budget bill generally allows a department to spend a specific amount—known as an "appropriation"—from the state treasury for a one-year period starting on July 1. The language making the appropriation matters: It can direct departments and limit managerial discretion. The Legislature and governor have fairly broad discretion about how they construct an appropriation. For example, spending authority can be specifically allocated among a department's activities, thereby limiting the department's discretion to reallocate funds among different programs. Or the appropriation can be made as a lump sum for all activities, providing the department broad administrative latitude to shift money among its various responsibilities.

American budgeting trends and practices are often seen to originate from a federal model. Perhaps this is why the public finance literature references federal practices. To be sure, the history of American public budgeting can be told as if federal budget practices evolved sequentially, as congressional emphasis in constructing budgets shifted from facilitating operational control to extending managerial authority and finally to encouraging planning.

Stage 1: Make Appropriations to Facilitate Operational Control

In this stage, Congress and the executive write the appropriation to ensure that specific tasks or functions are performed and that expenditures can be readily tracked and audited. By constructing appropriations in this way, elected officials use the budget to specify the purchase of specific objects, such as the purchase of 10 desks. Specific expenditures are recorded and then can be audited to ensure that funds were used as intended. In the wake of this type of budgeting, accounting systems and audit standards developed to reduce the occasions of fraud.

Decisions on funding levels, under this type of appropriation, will emphasize accounting and fiduciary responsibilities.

Stage 2: Make Appropriations to Enhance Management Authority

The appropriations made in this stage are intended to ensure that managers both receive sufficient resources to meet programmatic expectations and use broad discretion to accomplish organizational objectives. If successful, this style of appropriation will encourage managers to achieve greater efficiency within the budget allocation.

In this stage, Congress encourages departmental managers to innovate and pursue efficiencies because it had established sufficient audit and accounting control to protect the state from fraud and misappropriation.

This system promotes the development of workload measures and the evaluation of performance.

Instead of specifying objects to be purchased, as under the first stage, the budget bill reflects expenditures for programs, where object expenditures could be aggregated. Program managers were held accountable for how well their programs performed, rather than being asked to account for how many desks they purchased.

Stage 3: Making Appropriations to Improve Planning

In this stage, the appropriation is intended to help budget writers determine the scope and evolution of a department's objectives. If successful, it identifies not only the spending used to attain these objectives, but the policies to govern the use of public funds.[4] Decisions in this stage reflect an understanding of policy dynamics and objectives. This type of budgeting is said to have come to the fore in the mid-20th century, as information-processing technologies became ubiquitous and policy analysis tools developed. Given the ability to summarize and analyze budgeting patterns and economic conditions, budget-writers used the budget as a means to enhance and facilitate policymaking. In doing so, they linked spending decisions with the attainment of policy goals

(The proposals to modernize and change the federal budget were contained in a report from the federal Hoover Commission, named after the former president. California created its own budget and efficiency group explicitly modelled after the federal Hoover Commission. Colloquially given the informal diminutive, "Little Hoover Commission," it is officially named the Milton Marks Commission after a long-serving senator from San Francisco. To this day, the state commission continues to research and comment on ways to improve state finances.)

In this third stage, budget writers—both executive and legislative—explicitly use the budget to achieve policy in ways not possible or intended in the other stages. Schick describes making appropriations in this manner as recognizing the "latent policy opportunities" when making the budget.[5]

The budget appropriations in each of these stages are often described as if the task and routine for each type is distinct. It can seem that each stage is sequentially implemented in different budgets, and exclusive of the others. In practice, this history overstates the differences among the types. All budgets must ensure against fraud, promote efficiency, and encourage planning simultaneously. Budget makers do not have the luxury of constructing the budget sequentially. The history helps clarify a typology of appropriations. In practice, all three goals are present in budget decisions and are reflected in the budget bill.

---

[4] Allen Schick, "The Road to PPB: The Stages of Budget Reform," *Public Administration Review* 26 (December 1966): 243–58.

[5] *Ibid.*, 58.

Rarely, if ever, can a single budget emphasize all three goals equally. Generally, one goal dominates the other two. Typically, one type of appropriation style will predominate. Even so, they cannot be achieved in equal measure in all departments in a given year. Indeed, in a budget as large as California's it is unlikely that all departments will be budgeted in the same way. The Legislature or governor may be reluctant to give certain departments managerial latitude, so their budget will not reflect a management orientation.

The style and content of appropriations tell the department what the budget writers care about. They indicate the amount, use, accountability, and efficiency of spending.

Where Did the State Spend the General Fund in 2007–08?

In 2007–08, California spent an estimated $103.6 billion on state programs and local assistance. Traditionally, most of these expenditures are accounted for in five broad program areas: kindergarten through 12th grade and community college[6] (K-14), higher education, health, social services, and corrections. In 2007–08, and as displayed in Table 4.1, the state spent $82.1 billion (79.2 percent) from the General Fund on these program areas.

Kindergarten through High School

The Legislature allocated the majority of the General Fund to public schools for providing education to 6 million pupils in kindergarten through 12th grade in 2007–08. K-12 schools received a dedicated portion of the local property tax revenues to finance their operations, about $15.0 billion.

Higher Education

The state funded the California State University and University of California systems at about $6.0 billion.

Health and Human Services

Health and human services programs received the next largest share of the state budget, spending about $29.3 billion. Medi-Cal received about $14.1 billion from the General Fund. The costs of the Medi-Cal program are shared with the federal government. As such, eligibility requirements are primarily set by state and

---

[6] Department of Finance, Schedule 6, Governor's Budget 2009 (Sacramento: Calif.)

Table 4.1. General Fund Expenditures, by Major Category, Estimated in November 2008[a] (Dollars in Millions)

2007–08		
K-14[b]		36,241
Higher Education		
CSU	2,909	
UC	3,098	
Student Aid Commission	843	
Subtotal, Higher Education		6,850
Health and Human Services		
Medi-Cal	14,124	
CalWORKs	1,550	
SSI/SSP	3,659	
In Home Supportive Services	1,666	
Developmental Services	2,546	
Mental Health	1,941	
Other Health & Human Services	3,884	
Subtotal, Health & Human Services		29,370
Corrections and Rehabilitation		9,678
Judiciary		2,236
Proposition 42 Transfer		1,403
Debt Service on Infrastructure Bonds		4,264
Vehicle License Backfill[c]		5,704
Other Programs		7,893
Total		**103,639**

[a] Legislative Analyst Office, California's Fiscal Outlook (Sacramento, Calif., November 2008), 26.

[b] Does not include allocation for backfill of Vehicle License Fee transaction. This allocation is accounted for separately, see footnote c

[c] Estimate per Michael Coleman, *VLF Facts: A Primer on the Motor Vehicle In Lieu Tax.* www.californiacityfinance.com

federal laws, but eligibility is determined by county workers. Most of the program is administered at the local level.

Though the Department of Developmental Services has the second-largest claim on health spending from the General Fund, it receives much less than the Medi-Cal program. It received about $2.6 billion from the General Fund in 2007–

08, and serves individuals with developmental disabilities. Most of this funding, about $2.2 billion, is allocated to community programs. Vendors contract with the state to provide services in regional centers.

The Healthy Families Program enables lower-income families to purchase low-cost health coverage for their children if they are unable to qualify for Medi-Cal. The state and federal government subsidize the insurance, thereby making health insurance, including coverage for vision, dental, and mental health, available to working families. The program is administered by the state's Managed Risk Medical Insurance Board, and the state provides $390 million of the program's total cost of about $1.0 billion.

The Department of Mental Health received $1.9 billion in 2007–08. The bulk of this spending, around $1.0 billion, is allocated for the operation of state hospitals. The state provided local governments, mostly counties, with mental health assistance totalling about $300 million.

The biggest social services program is the Supplemental Security Income/State Supplementary Program (SSI/SSP). It received $3.7 billion.

The next largest social services program, California Work Opportunity and Responsibility to Kids (CalWORKs), is the state's primary welfare program. It emerged from the Legislature's 1997 welfare reform efforts, and received $1.6 billion.

General Fund support for the In-Home Supportive Services program totalled nearly $1.7 billion in 2007–08. This program provides in-home care for the aged, blind, and disabled. Often, the assistance provided through the program is an alternative to placing the clients in nursing homes, which are more expensive.

The other social programs, including child welfare and child support services, received $3.9 billion from the General Fund.

Criminal Justice

Corrections and justice programs received about $11.9 billion from the General Fund. By far, the state's prison system received the largest share of this funding. The Department of Corrections and Rehabilitation received about $9.7 billion.

Debt Payments

Debt payments include the General Fund appropriation to service the General Fund's short- and long-term borrowings. The debt payments pay the annual incremental cost for servicing general obligation and lease-revenue bonds.

The final category of spending listed in Table 4.1 is "Other Programs," a rather poor descriptor of programs. It serves as a catchall for programs not itemized. The biggest component of this category is General Fund contributions to public retirement systems. For the year, the state allocated $4.6 billion, a 21 percent increase from the prior year. This was mostly related to a one-time increase resulting from a court order for the state to pay the teacher's retirement system for a deferred retirement contribution. The balance of the costs in this category is associated with funding for the state's constitutional officers, tax systems, and resources and environmental programs.[7]

This review of a particular year, while providing a snapshot of spending, will tend to oversimplify the budget, as it reflects the fiscal and political conditions of a particular year.

Changes in Spending over Time

Another way to put spending in context is to review changes in spending patterns over time. Table 4.2[8] compares spending from 1998–99 to 2007–08. This period is more limited than the one used in the revenue chapter because the Legislature adopted two significant programmatic changes that reduce the comparability of current spending patterns and those from the mid-1990s. First, the Legislature made a dramatic change in school funding sources in the early 1990s shifting property tax revenue to schools from cities, counties, and special districts. This shift in revenue streams reduced state spending for schools while increasing local spending. While schools did not receive a greater amount of overall revenues, local governments lost billions of dollars from their property tax streams. It would be distracting and confusing to include school financing prior to these shifts unless the analysis were to include the overall effect on local programs. Such an analysis is beyond the scope of this chapter.

Second, the state responded in 1997 to federal welfare reform, which eliminated the state's Aid to Families with Dependent Children and instituted the Cal WORKs program. As this change was so large a break with prior state/federal spending relationships, this chapter concentrates on spending patterns beginning in 1997–98.

Even the limited, nine-year comparison of spending patterns shows changes in the way the state spends the General Fund. Between 1998-99 and 2007-08, annual spending grew from $58.6 billion to $103.6 billion, an increase of about $45.6 billion. Proposition 98 and Medi-Cal received $11.5 billion and $7.1 billion, respectively, of the increase. As the largest two spending categories, these programs would be expected to exhibit large increases. But their growth rate was not as fast as other programs.

The average annual growth rate for all spending was about was about 6.5 percent. But not all programs grew at the same rate. As displayed in Table 4.2, the allocations for the backfill in the vehicle license fee, Medi-Cal and Correc-

---

[7] At the time this book was written, the governor and Legislature were considering reopening the 2008–09 budget to reduce spending.

[8] California Debt and Investment Advisory Commission, GO Debt Trends 2008 (Sacramento, Calif.).

Table 4.2. Change in General Fund Spending by Major Program, 1998–99 and 2007–08 (Dollars in Millions)

	1998–99[a]	2007–08[b]	Change Total over Period	Average Annual
K-14	$24,773	$36,241	$11,468	4.3%
Medi-Cal	7,026	14,124	7,098	8.1%
Corrections	3,721	9,678	5,957	11.2%
VLF[c]	557	5,704	5,147	29.5%
Higher Education	4,505	6,850	2,345	4.8%
Debt Service	2,355	4,264	1,909	6.8%
Proposition 42	-	1,403	1,403	N/A
SSI/SSP	2,244	3,659	1,415	5.6%
CalWORKs	2,025	1,550	-475	-2.9%
Other Programs	11,373	20,166	8,793	6.6%
Totals	$58,579	$103,639	$45,060	6.5%

[a] 1998–99 figures per Legislative Analyst's Office, California's Fiscal Outlook, November 1999.

[b] 2007–08 figures per Legislative Analyst's Office, California''s Fiscal Outlook, November 2008.

[c] VLF estimate per Michael Coleman, VLF Facts: A Primer on the Motor Vehicle in Lieu Tax. www.californiacityfinance.com

tions grew at a much faster annual rate than the rest of the budget. Allocations for K-14 and CalWORKs grew at rates below the overall average annual growth rate.

Did allocations keep up with changes in costs and inflation? The far right column in Table 4.3 identifies how much spending rose or fell during the period, after accounting for inflation and population. For some programs, appropriations seem to have stayed even with cost pressures. In other cases, such as for Cal-WORKs, spending fell significantly relative to inflation. Is this because there was a lower demand for services? Did the Legislature and governor change the program to reduce eligibility and assistance?

Other categories grew at a rate much faster than inflation and population alone. This was true of Corrections, Medi-Cal payments, and the payments to local governments for their loss of VLF revenue. While this analysis leads to the conclusion that the state is shifting its General Fund spending away from schools and

Table 4.3. Change in General Fund Spending by Major Program Adjustments for Inflation and Population, 1998–99 and 2007–08 (Dollars in Millions)

| | 1998–99 [a] | 2007–08 [b] | Growth 1998–99 through 2007–08 | | |
			Actual Growth	Growth with General Inflation and Population [c, d,]	Actual Infl + Pop
K-14	$24,773	$36,241	$ 11,468	$37,134	-$893
Medi-Cal	7,026	14,124	7,098	10,532	3,592
Corrections	3,721	9,678	5,957	5,578	4,100
VLF [e]	557	5,704	5,147	835	4,869
Higher Education	4,505	6,850	2,345	6,753	97
Debt Service	2,355	4,264	1,909	3,530	734
Proposition 42	-	1,403	1,403	0	1,403
SSI/SSP	2,244	3,659	1,415	3,364	295
CalWORKs	2,025	1,550	-475	3,035	-1,485
Other Programs	11,373	20,166	8,793	17,048	$3,118
Totals	58,579	103,639	45,060	$87,807	$15,832

[a] 1998–,99 figures per Legislative Analyst's Office, California's Fiscal Outlook, November 1999.

[b] 2007–08 figures per Legislative Analyst's Office, California's Fiscal Outlook, November 2008.

[c] Inflation estimate January to January CPI-U, per U.S. Department of Labor.

[d] Population estimate, Department of Finance, *Governor's Budget,* 2009 Schedule 6.

[e] 2007–08 VLF figure from Michael Coleman.

toward corrections, VLF and Medi-Cal, a broader analysis might include specific program indices. For example, though Medi-Cal is growing at a rate faster than inflation, that growth might reflect the fact that medical costs are growing at rates at least twice as fast as general inflation, so the program will have to grow faster to maintain service levels over time. K-12 schools, while losing their share of the General Fund, will be able to maintain service levels as long as they grow with inflation and enrollment.

Complexity and Breadth of Spending
Make Consensus Difficult

If the Legislature were to heed the governor's call to reduce spending, how would it know where to cut? There is no formula for identifying nonessential services. Often, the "essentialness" of a program is in the eye of the beholder. Sometimes, budget writers appeal to the work of economists to construct a welfare function for public spending. After the social scientist V. O. Key formulated the challenge in a 1940 article,[9] much work has been done to try to find a practical way to allocate rationally "x dollars to activity A instead of activity B." Relying on the conceptual framework of marginal returns, there is a seductive appeal to the idea that the Legislature could, if enough information were available, allocate every tax dollar to its highest and best use, such that the last program funded is the highest priority among all other possible uses of the last available dollar.

Alas, no science can easily replace the subjective nature of budget choices. College students may want the last dollar to be invested in the university systems, while new parents may prefer increased funding for child care programs or class size reduction in elementary schools. Others may prefer tax relief to additional spending.

Much of the state's finances are intertwined with local and federal budget conditions. When the federal government reduces its support for transportation operations, the state has to pick up the difference or let roads and transit systems erode. In practice, the ability to finance government services is part of a network of funding from federal, state, and local sources. When local governments face budget shortfalls, often based on erosion of the tax bases they share with the state, they are unable to provide certain services, thereby putting pressure on state spending.

Even if the state's economy and revenue base remains stable, when the federal budget is under stress, federal spending may fall. The state may then have to assume a greater responsibility for funding shared programs.

Californians have a hard time evaluating or providing context for these changes. As a result, California's debate about whether the state spends "too much" cannot be measured or documented beyond the broadest characterizations. The debate is not likely to be resolved by referring to funding levels from any particular year or years. There is a suspicion that a particular year's spending is conditioned on that year's peculiar fiscal or political conditions. Appropriation levels provide no information about whether the levels serve the needs and expectations of the state. It is rather more likely that Californians will be persuaded by a careful consideration of whether the authorized spending is likely to meet the state's needs. Will it do so in the future? There are two dimensions to this.

---

[9] V. O. Key, "The Lack of a Budgetary Theory," *The American Political Science Review* XXXIV (1940): 1138.

1. Adequate Measures to Evaluate the Use of Spending

California Forward, a broad-based public interest coalition, recommends that the state articulate standards for programmatic or departmental activities. These standards should translate into actions taken. Do those actions meet the performance measures? Are departments achieving articulated goals?

If not, what is preventing them? Can management be improved? Is funding sufficient?

2. Affordability

Spending cannot be measured in the abstract, but only in the context of available resources and the perceived needs of the state. Since spending "demand" will likely always exceed available revenues, was the available revenue put to the best use? Can the need be reduced or redefined? Can revenues be increased?

Conclusion

State spending has been on a long-standing, upward trend, even as the allocations among programs have changed significantly over time. When Governor Schwarzenegger declared the state's ongoing budget problem a "spending" problem, he tried to focus the budget debate on the outflow of General Fund money. Perhaps he will be more successful than his predecessors when negotiating a "cuts only" budget.

To be sure, the governor and Legislature face continued pressure to reduce General Fund allocations. As described in this chapter, they can exercise controls over how appropriations are made and how spending is evaluated. Given the complexity and breadth of state spending, it is probably futile to attempt some systemic review of all state spending. As a document developed through consensus, the budget bill reflects a collective judgment from the executive and legislative branches about spending priorities and the state's needs. By itemizing thousands of individual funding decisions, the budget includes thousands of reasons for critics to oppose the entire document. Each appropriation represents a reason to vote against the entire budget bill. Does the budget provide enough funding for nursing homes? Does it spend too much on incarcerating criminals? It would be expedient to vote against an entire budget if one disagreed with any particular decision. To the extent it reflects a working consensus it also contains the state's commitments to public service. While state spending remains over time mostly associated with schools, health, social, and corrections programs, the share of funds allocated to each of these broad programs evolved over the last 10 years. There are many reasons for this, including changing interests, cost pressures, and caseloads.

To broaden appreciation of the rigidity of state spending or the need for continuing spending, the state would be well served to seek consensus among Californians about the kind of analytical measures used to assess and monitor budget allocations and performance.

Chapter 5

The State's Fiscal Equation: Debt, Accounting, and "Off Budget" Solutions

The last two chapters reviewed the pattern of state expenditures and revenues. When the state runs a budget deficit, it is generally assumed that either expenditures will be cut or taxes increased. In practice, the Legislature and governor can engage in a wide array of budget-balancing methods. What are their alternatives and how should Californians evaluate them? This chapter catalogues the more common practices and provides a context in which they can be evaluated for their consequences. Most of the techniques are an effective way of shifting costs, mostly in the form of higher debt costs to future taxpayers.

Evaluating a Budget as a Financial Plan

At their core, budgets serve as a kind of financial plan to identify how the state pays for services (including those services provided each year over the life of capital projects, such as roads and buildings with a useful life of 30 years). Central to the notion of using the budget as a financial plan is the presumed necessity of "balancing" revenues and expenditures in any fiscal year. "Balance" in this context can be described as the identity Revenues = Expenditures. Bringing "Expenditure" to the left side of this equation yields the expression:

Equation 1   *Revenues − Expenditures = 0*

In practice, the governor and Legislature find it hard to exactly match revenues and expenditures, so they expect that the difference between revenue and expenditures will be positive, such that:

Equation 2 $Revenues - Expenditures \geq 0$

The last two chapters reviewed the expenditures detailed in the state budget and the revenues that finance them. To be sure, these are the two major components of the state's fiscal structure, as budgets in deficit are generally "balanced" by either cutting expenditures or raising revenues. When the Legislature and the governor cannot agree on a compromise that would cut spending or raise taxes, they have resorted to other methods for balancing the budget.

These equations are in the same spirit as the constitutional provision prohibiting the state's Legislature from creating

> . . . any debt or debts, liability or liabilities, which shall, singly or in the aggregate with any previous debts or liabilities, exceed the sum of three hundred thousand dollars ($300,000).

This prohibition, contained in Section 1 of Article XVI of the state constitution and known as the "debt clause," has been read to prevent the Legislature from paying for this year's costs with tax dollars received in later years. It would seem to require the Legislature to spend no more than it takes in. As such, by constraining spending to whatever taxpayers were willing and able to pay, the debt clause could act as a powerful spending limit.

The debt clause also seems to promote what public finance experts sometimes refer to as "intergenerational equity." Treating each year's set of taxpayers as a collective with a common interest in financing and receiving government services, each group can be thought of as a unique "cohort" to whom the costs and benefits of government services accrue. By requiring each year's cohort of taxpayers to pay for the services they receive, the debt clause seems to prohibit fiscal policies that allow one set of taxpayers to beggar a later cohort.

Put another way, the debt clause seems to require that the "average" Californian receive no more in services than he or she pays for in any given year. By balancing revenues and expenses, the Legislature ensures that each taxpayer cohort may be said to be "fair" to future taxpayers who neither benefit nor have a say in the amount of taxes they will have imposed. There may be other ways of measuring equity, including equity between taxpayer cohorts—or indeed within a taxpayer cohort—but these measures of equity are not bounded by the constraint imposed by Equation 2 or the constitution.

At times, the state has balanced its budget within the constraints imposed by Equation 2. For example in 1999–00, the state generated $70.0[1] billion in General Fund taxes and spent $66.5 billion, for a tax surplus of about $3.5 billion.[2]

---

[1] Department of Finance, Governor's Budget 2009, Schedules 2 and 6.

Though General Fund tax revenues exceeded expenditures in 1999-00, in each year since then the state spent more than it took in, generating a tax deficit for each year since 2000-01. For example, in 2000-01, the state spent $78.1 billion, while it took in $75.7 billion, and therefore spent $2.1 billion more than it took in. Please see Table 5.1.

Californians find their state government running chronic tax deficits—despite constitutional prohibitions, equity concerns, and public finance theory. The persistence of the tax deficit begs the question: How does the state finance its budget in the face of continued shortfalls in tax revenues? After it exhausts its reserves, as it did in 2001–02, the state may seek "nontax revenues," such as revenue from the sale of state property. When it sells an asset, such as unused real estate, it deposits the sale proceeds in the General Fund. These revenues, not directly dervied from a tax levy, are available to the Legislature for financing General Fund expenditures.

What happens if, after the state uses all its tax and "nontax" revenues, it still has insufficient revenue? In recent years, it has turned to borrowing for filling the difference between expenditures and revenues. To account for this possibility, Equation 2 can be expanded to include debt, such that:

Equation 3   *(Revenue + Debt) – Expenditures ≥ 0*

Equation 3 presumes that this debt is typically short- or medium-term in nature. Mostly, the borrowing is for a period of less than a year, but the electorate can authorize a longer term. The Legislature employs many different methods for this kind of borrowing. Sometimes, as in 2004, the Legislature asks voters to approve the issuance of a bond to finance prior deficits. This bond, approved by the voters in November 2004, authorized the state to issue a bond of up to $15 billion to be financed over a seven-year period. This debt, approved directly by the voters, authorized the 2004–05 budget to be balanced with the allocation of the proceeds from the bond.

Beyond voter-approved debt, the state may borrow by other means. For example, for the 2008–09 budget, the Legislature required taxpayers "to accelerate" their tax payments. That is, taxpayers prepayed their tax and thereby shifted tax payments from 2009–10 to 2008–09. This is a way of taking taxes due in the next year and making them available for spending earlier. It is a way of making next year pay for this year's services. It is believed that such an acceleration does not violate the constitutional prohibition on debt, however.

Often, the state borrows deeply from its own funds outside the General Fund. On June 30, 2008, the Department of Finance reported that the General Fund had

---

[2] Typically, discussions of the state's financial condition center on the General Fund balance. The state deposits the proceeds of broad taxes, notably the personal income tax and the sales tax, into the General Fund. General Fund revenues are not earmarked for any particular program or service, so the Legislature may allocate these revenues to a broad cross-section of government programs and services, including public schools, prisons, and state parks.

**Table 5.1. Comparison of General Fund Tax Collections and
Expenditures 1999–00 through 2007–08 (Dollars in Billions)**

	1999–00	2000–01	2001–02	2002–03
Expenditures	$ 66.5	$ 78.1	$ 76.8	$77.5
Tax Collections	70.0	75.7	62.7	64.9
Difference	$3.5	-$2.4	-$14.1	-$12.6

	2003–04	2004–05	2005–06	2006–07
Expenditures	$ 78.3	$ 79.8	$ 91.6	$ 101.4
Tax Collections	70.2	80.1	90.5	93.2
Difference	-$8.1	$0.3	-$1.1	-$8.2

Source: Department of Finance. Schedules 2 and 6, *Governor's Budget Summary 2009–10* (Sacramento, Calif.: Department of Finance). Totals may not add due to rounding.

borrowed over $950 million from assorted special funds, including the bottles and cans recycling fund, the Public Utilities Commission, the dental board, the accountancy board, and the Department of Housing and Community Development. These "loans," as the Legislature constructs them, are considered outside the constitutional debt provisions.

The state can also borrow from private investors on a short-term basis without voter approval. Under certain circumstances, rather vaguely permitted by judicial interpretation, borrowing can be incurred without violating the debt clause prohibition.

The state may issue debt in two ways to manage its short-term finances without compromising its long-term fiscal health.

1. Cash Flow

It may use short-term debt to match monthly expenses and income; that is, it may borrow in order to meet its cash flow needs. The state collects its General Fund revenues in fits and starts during the year. For example, the state's predominate revenue source, the personal income tax, is due in full on April 15. While many taxpayers pay a portion of their taxes through withholding, about one-third of the income tax is paid in mid-April—after 75 percent of the fiscal year has passed. Though revenues may be episodic, state expenses tend to be more continuous, so there is a mismatch between outflows and inflows during the year. In particular, the state's first fiscal quarter (from July 1 through September 30) is a lean revenue quarter. To cover expenses during these "lean" revenue periods, the state may borrow for a time until the revenues are paid.

2. Economic Cycles

The state's tax system responds to the economy. When employment is high and incomes are growing, the state experiences healthy revenue streams. During recessions, tax streams will be more anemic. During these economic contractions, the state can expect economic recovery, so the Legislature may not want to make permanent reductions in its spending patterns. Legislators may conclude, in fact, that it is even more important during recessions to provide full assistance to Californians. Rather than create dislocations in programs and services, the Legislature and governor may decide to borrow to keep services at prerecession levels and protect those dependent on services. However, the state's recent history of deficit financing has been sustained through an upward tick in the business cycle.

For these two short-term phenomena, the state might wish to borrow to balance its budget in any given year. In both cases, the state's long-term balance between revenues and expenditures are not a consideraiton. The short-term conditions in Equation 3 are fulfilled.

Long-Term Debt Is Different

When the state issues longer-term debt, such as a 30-year general obligation bond, the analysis changes. The state deposits the proceeds into a bond fund for allocation by the Legislature. The borrowed money is allocable in a single year or over many years, even though the bondholders will be repaid over the life of a bond.

The state repays the bondholders over the term of the bond with annual appropriations from the General Fund. The direct price for borrowing in any given year, therefore, is the cost of paying the bondholders, known as paying the "debt service."

The state uses the proceeds of debt to finance its capital, such as structures and property acquisition. For the period 2001–02, the state issued $70.3 billion in debt. Education facilities, primarily K-12 school districts, received $35.6 billion (51 percent) of this debt financing. The state allocated another $14.3 billion (20 percent) to housing, while issuing $6.6 billion (nine percent) for health facilities. The state sold the remaining amount, about $13.8 billion, to finance all its other capital projects for the period. Table 5.2 displays a year-by-year breakdown of issued bonds by major purpose. Long-term debt does not show up in the General Fund budget equation, except as debt service.

There are two practical considerations for evaluating this long-term debt. First, does the debt practice reflect spending priorities? According to the legislative analyst, debt service costs will grow from $3.9 billion to $7.7 billion between 2008–09 and 2013–14. This is an average annual growth rate of 12.2 percent, by

John Decker

Table 5.2. Bonds Issued for Financing Capital By Major Purpose and Year, 2001 through 2005 (Dollars in Millions)

	2001-02	2002-03	2003-04	2004-05
Health	$ 512	$ 414	$ 1,074	$ 1,716
Housing	2,176	2,110	2,628	2,621
Education	3,199	3,527	8,895	5,571
Other Capital	1,442	2,880	3,052	3,073
Totals	$ 7,329	$ 8,931	$ 15,649	$12,981

	2005-06	2006-07	2001-02 through 2006-07	
			Amount	Percent
Health	$ 1,583	$ 1,305	$ 6,604	9%
Housing	2,707	2,059	14,301	20%
Education	8,775	5,639	35,606	51%
Other Capital	2,038	1,302	13,787	20%
Totals	$ 15,103	$ 10,305	$ 70,298	

far the fastest growing aspect of the budget. The analyst expects total General Fund spending to grow at less than half that rate, about 5.4 percent.

If the Legislature permits debt service costs to grow faster than other programs, then Californians may rightly view debt costs as the priority call on new spending. For them to evaluate whether this is the appropriate priority, they might consider two policy issues:

- How cost-effective are the capital projects acquired through the use of debt? Will they produce a return that exceeds their cost? Do they produce the highest return among alternative capital projects?
- Is capital acquisition the highest priority for the money spent? Or, should other programs or services have a higher claim on this money?

In these ways, when Californians evaluate the debt service spending, they can evaluate both the use of capital spending and whether it is most appropriate to allocate the funds to infrastructure or operating expenses. To answer these questions, the Legislature will have to set standards for the amount of long-term debt it approves and the kinds of facilities it finances with debt.

The second practical consideration can be whether long-term debt affects long-term fiscal health. Long-term borrowing locks-in state expenses for paying principal and interest over the life of the bond. Because the state must pay off the loan it cannot easily reduce its debt-service costs. By committing to specific bond payments over the life of a bond (which may have a 30-year term), the borrowing locks in a specific amount of annual outflow for servicing the debt. It thereby limits its flexibility to reduce or manage costs in each of the budgets during the term of the bond.

Plumping Up the June 30th Balance

Typically, the press and the Department of Finance measure whether the state fulfills the conditions of Equation 3 by assessing the balance by June 30, the end of the fiscal year. By checking the balance on that same date each year, some believe that the state has a consistent year-by-year measure of inflow and outgo. It is a practical measure, irrespective of other daily cash balances, and seems consistent with the construct of Equation 3. It offers a comforting assurance that the state's fiscal condition can be measured and assessed with some certainty.

Though the June 30 "balance" is a simple and practical, even intuitive, measure of budget soundness, it is easily manipulated. For example, if the state's accounts are in deficits during the days before and after June 30, how confident can Californians feel that the budget is a "sound" financial plan? Consider the budget the governor signed for the 2008–09 fiscal year. His Department of Finance estimated that the June 30, 2009, balance would be about $2.6 billion. As a financial plan, however, the 2008–09 budget provided little comfort that the state managed its accounts responsibly. Though the Department of Finance estimated that the budget would end the year with a surplus, it acknowledged even as the governor signed the bill that in each subsequent year the state's revenue structure could not sustain the spending at levels authorized in 2008–09. Each year starting in 2009–10, the state would run deficits, and that each year the deficits would compound.

In practice, the Legislature and governor have learned to use an array of methods for propping up the balance, if only for purposes of making a positive accounting on June 30 of each year. To raise end-of-year General Fund balances they have included borrowed resources, deferred paying off current-accounts, made accounting changes, and transferred money from non-General Fund accounts. The methods, catalogued below, do not neatly fit into the construct assumed in Equation 3, as they do not explicitly raise revenues, increase debt services payments, or cut expenditures. Though often derided as "gimmicks" or "tricks," they nevertheless have become an essential part of the state's budgeting.

Method 1: Defer Payments

In general, a private party cannot demand the state pay it for services rendered unless the Legislature has both authorized the contract and appropriated funds. There are, however, certain payments that must be made, even without an appropriation. For example, the constitution requires the state to pay local governments for their costs of complying with the provisions of state law. Starting in 1992, the Legislature did not make a full appropriation for these yearly mandated costs. Instead, the Legislature informed local governments that they would be paid in later years—that is, in arrears—for these mandated costs. The Legislature deferred even more payments in subsequent years, and the amount owed to local governments accumulated, finally exceeding half a billion dollars. By "deferring" the payments the Legislature reduced its costs in any given fiscal year, even as it was pushing costs into future budgets. (Voters limited this practice in 2004 when they approved a constitutional amendment requiring the Legislature to make timely payments for these costs.)

In addition, the Legislature has discretion to defer other annual costs. When the state loses a judicial decision, the court may order the state to make payments to the winning party. But, in those years when it found its finances constrained, the Legislature deferred making court-ordered payments.

The state can also underestimate its likely costs as a way of reducing appropriations in the budget bill. When constructing the 2000–01, 2001–02 and 2002–03 budgets, the Legislature adopted programmatic reforms of the state's prison system. Each year, the Legislature passed—and the governor signed—"reform legislation" that was estimated to reduce annual costs by as much as $1 billion. In practice, the "savings" were fictional and never materialized. But by reducing the prison budget by an amount assumed to be generated in the legislation, the Legislature could "balance" the budget. When the "reforms" did not produce the savings and prison costs rose above budgeted levels, the budget totals became unbalanced.

In another example, the state makes two annual payments to the state's retirement system to fund employee retirement benefits. When the Legislature slipped the second annual payment into the next fiscal year, it skipped a pension payment in that year and in so doing, it halved the cost of benefit payments for a year.

The Legislature can "defer" paying for costs in any given year through many budgetary devices. It can explicitly choose to push costs into another budget or it can simply fail to recognize the full costs for government. Either way, the Legislature does not eliminate any costs, but temporarily addresses the state's balance by shifting costs to later budgets or other funding streams.

Method 2: Accelerate Revenues

The Legislature can change the due date for taxes and thereby move tax payments into earlier fiscal years. For example, in 2008, the state required taxpayers to prepay their personal income taxes and corporation taxes. By advancing the state's personal income tax withholding schedules and advancing the timing for when estimated corporate tax payments were due, the Legislature was able to move tax payments from later fiscal years into the 2008–09 budget. It raised 2008–09 General Fund revenues by over $2.5 billion by requiring these accelerations.

Accelerations are popular because they do not require an increase in taxes or a cut in expenditures when trying to finance a deficit. By requiring taxpayers to shift their taxes from next year to this year, however, the effect is to finance the cost of government from the cohort of taxpayers who would otherwise be paying for next year's services. Acceleration moves the burden of the deficit to next year's taxpayers.

Method 3: Adjust Accounting Practices

Within a certain latitude afforded by professional accounting standards, the state can adjust when it recognizes the payment of taxes or costs. By adjusting its accounting, the state has improved its fund balances without cutting spending or raising taxes. In 1991, it adopted an accounting standard, consistent with preferred national practices, that required the state to attribute all costs in the year they were incurred and all revenues in the year they were due. This accounting change meant that irrespective of when a cost was paid or a tax receipt collected, the state could record the fiscal effect of the transaction at the time the cost occurred or revenue was due. Making the change, the state increased its balance by recognizing the receipt of revenues sooner and deferring when it recognized costs. The change in accounting allowed the state—on a one-time basis—to recognize more revenue due than costs incurred for 1991–92 than it would have under its prior accounting system. This accounting change allowed the state to improve its balance sheet by over $1 billion in 1991–92.

Though the accounting change was considered a prudent and responsible change in budgeting practices, as it encouraged a strict accounting of revenues and expenses attributable to each year, in later years the state reversed itself on the accounting basis for a select number of transactions. In 2003–04, it accounted for Medi-Cal payments on an actual—rather than accrual—basis, thereby allowing the state to book the cost of Medi-Cal payments when paid. Since the state pays in arrears, this accounting change allowed the state to recognize a one-time reduction in costs for 2003–04 of about $2 billion. It did so by merely pushing costs into subsequent years.

Method 4: Transfer Special Fund Revenue to the General Fund

State tax policy distinguishes between the levy of "general" taxes and "special" taxes. The distinction grew from a phrase used, but not defined, in Proposition 13. That proposition, approved by voters in 1978, required that "special taxes" be imposed with a two-thirds vote of the electorate, saying:

> Cities, counties and special districts, by a two-thirds vote of the qualified electors of such district may impose special taxes on such districts, except ad valorem

taxes on real property or a transactions tax or sales tax on the sale of real property within such city, county or special district.

The term "special tax" had no accepted meaning in public finance at the time, nor was it defined by the initiative. As a result, a key provision of the proposition was left to judicial interpretation. The appellate court in San Francisco considered the term "special tax" to be distinguished from other taxes,[3] saying

[we] are asked to read the word "special" out of the phrase "special taxes," in violation of settled rules of construction and in the face of the language of Section 3 which indicates that the drafters knew how to say "any" taxes when that is what they meant. Our choice here is not simply between acceptance of one of a number of different meanings of an ambiguous term in a statute, but between disregarding the word "special" altogether in Section 4 or affording its some meaning consistent with the intent of the voters in enacting the provision. . . . In keeping with these principles we constitute the term "special taxes" in Section 4 to mean taxes which are levied for a specific purpose, rather than as in the present case, a levy placed in the general fund to be utilized for general governmental purposes.[4]

Proposition 62, approved by the voters in 1986, codified the *Farrell* definition and added the requirement that "general" taxes may only be imposed by a majority popular vote.[5] Proceeds of special taxes and other exactions may be used to offset General Fund expenditures.

Using these offsetting revenues allows the Legislature to reduce General Fund expenditures and improve its General Fund balance. However, because other fees, assessments, or exactions fill the special funds, the cost of government programs is not eliminated. The cost is simply shifted from the General Fund to special funds.

Method 5: Use Local Revenue for State Purposes

Cities, counties, special districts, and school districts all receive a portion of the property tax. When Proposition 13 passed, it limited the countywide property tax rate to one percent, but did not identify who would allocate the revenue generated at this rate. The Legislature has assumed the responsibility for allocating the property tax, as school financing is a state responsibility and is financed with a combination of property tax revenue and state General Fund revenue. As the

---

[3] City and County of San Francisco v Farrell.

[4] Peter Detwiler, Leslie McFadden, Dave Doerr, Ellen Worcester, Martin Helmke, and Anne Maitland, "Proposition 62: Analysis of Issues and Provisions" (Sacramento, Calif.: Senate Publications, September 1986).

[5] Martin Helmke and John Decker, "Proposition 136—Taxpayers Right to Vote," August 15, 1990 page 7. Contained in Senate Committee on Revenue and Taxation, Joint Hearing on Proposition 129, 133, 134 and 136, August 15, 1990 (Sacramento, Calif.: Senate Publications).

Legislature allocates more property tax to the schools it can reduce—on a dollar-for-dollar basis—the amount of General Fund revenue allocated to schools.

Since 1992, the Legislature has moved billions of dollars from cities, counties, and special districts to school districts and reduced General Fund appropriations by a commensurate amount. Through these transactions, state expenditures for schools fall and budget balance is restored. Though schools experienced no change in the amount allocated to them, the costs of funding the schools was shifted to the cities, counties, and special districts that lost revenue.

"Balance" Is Not Enough

A balance achieved within the provisions of Equation 3 presumes that an end-of-year positive balance is a singular consideration in crafting a budget. In the heat of a lengthy and bitter negotiation, the governor and Legislature may be excused for adopting stop-gap or expedient "off budget" measures. To help construct a deal, "off budget" solutions can provide welcome balance consistent with the conditions of Equation 3. Under the rubric of this equation, it is assumed that when the Legislature pursues an annual balance between current revenues and expenditures, it will generally adopt budgets ensuring that taxpayers in any year will pay for the services they receive. The balance requirement, in this way, is assumed to impose a certain amount of fiscal discipline. However, it is not a sufficient measure of prudence or soundness in budgeting. California's recent budgets provide ample evidence that the budget document is freighted with meanings beyond an accounting of revenues and expenditures. When a budget's "balance" is measured by whether the state's expenditures are equal to or less than available resources, the Legislature and governor may face strong incentives to mask fiscal problems.

The "off budget" methods, all used to achieve a balance on June 30, can be criticized as shifting costs but not eliminating them. These shifts may be from the current fiscal year to a later year, as when the Legislature defers payments, accelerates revenues, and makes certain accounting changes. "Off budget" methods can also be used to shift costs from one funding source to another, such as the practice of moving costs from the General Fund to state special funds or to local governments.

Sometimes, the nature and magnitude of these shifts are evident, such as when the state delays reimbursing local governments for their state-mandated costs. Other times, the effect is not so clear. For example, by shifting property tax revenue from cities to schools, the Legislature and governor redistribute the costs of school finance from the state General Fund to local property owners.

Critics complain that "off budget" methods are a kind of rouges' gallery of bad budget practices. To what extent are the methods pernicious? Are they irresponsible? How can Californians evaluate these alternative balancing schemes? Three measures help assess the effectiveness and appropriateness of these techniques.

1. Transparency

Many believe that transparency is an antiseptic that corrects the ills of government excess, including financial malpractice. They believe that "disclosure" and "open government" will either help insure against imprudent decisions or lead to a quick corrective. In a way, "transparent budgets" may be seen to limit the opportunity for making poor government decisions. By their nature, "off budget" methods limit the amount of information available to taxpayers.

Because off budget solutions may either understate the true cost of government or overstate the amount of revenue available for allocation in a given year, Californians will find it harder to track budget decisions and assess their consequences. For example, because of its obscure fiscal interactions, the effect of the "roundabout" maneuver described at the beginning of Chapter 2 is impossible to track except by the budget *cognoscenti*. More egregiously, the fiscal effect of the property tax shift was to increase school financing and cut local government's discretionary funds. Local governments had lower revenues, so they cut discretionary activities such as library hours and closed recreation facilities. But how is a taxpayer to track the effect of this transaction? How can the taxpayer be expected to understand that the neighborhood library closed to make sure that the state could pay its school bills?

2. Fairness

"Off budget" solutions shift costs. Are these cost shifts equitable or fair? There are at least two ways to measure "fairness" of fiscal policy. Assuming that the cohort of taxpayers that benefits should pay for its services, then "off budget" solutions can be evaluated as to whether they appropriately reallocate costs to the beneficiaries. In this sense, shifting the cost of park maintenance from the general taxpayer to a camper who pays an overnight park fee might improve fairness. A less-fair cost shift would result from deferring maintenance and having future taxpayers pay for the cost to maintain the campsite.

Another common measure of fairness is to allocate costs on the payer's "ability to pay." In this way, costs are distributed on the assumption that revenues are more "affordable" to wealthier payers. To the extent "off budget" solutions impose higher revenue liability on wealthier taxpayers (through the income tax system or through the taxation of "luxury items"), an "off budget" solution could be said to improve fairness. Rarely will "off budget" methods meet this criteria.

3. Sustainability

There is a reasonable expectation that a budget adopted in one year will not over-commit future resources. That is, the spending commitment made in today's budget will be financed in the future without an increase in the tax structure. By accelerating revenues, the Legislature temporarily inflates the amount of money available to pay the state's bills in a particular fiscal year. By shifting costs to later years, it increases beyond its current means the amount of services it can provide. The Legislature is explicitly constructing a budget that is unlikely to be balanced in future years.

A budget that balances current revenues and expenditures is a goal rarely met by the state of California. To ensure that the budget has a positive end-of-year balance, the Legislature relies increasingly on debt and a variety of "off budget" methods. These methods tend to shift costs to different cohorts of taxpayers, including fee-payers, future taxpayers, and local governments. Often derided as "gimmicks," these practices can diminish the soundness of the state's budget as a financial plan.

Chapter 6

California's Fiscal Structure

Outside the State Capitol in the darkening afternoon of December 8, 2008, workers had finished decorating the three-story holiday pine shipped in from the Sierra Nevada. As they checked the lights to make sure all was working prior to the official lighting ceremony, the tree was a cheery reminder of the coming holiday season. But the mood in the Capitol was anything but festive. The Assembly Speaker and the Senate President pro Tempore had convened a joint session of both houses in the Assembly chambers. They invited the state treasurer, state controller, director of the Department of Finance, and the legislative analyst to discuss the state's fiscal condition. Mike Genest, the state's finance director, told legislators that the state faced a growing deficit of more than $11 billion in the current year and $17 billion in the year after. The Legislature would have to find $28 billion worth of budget solutions (spending cuts, tax increases, or gimmicks) between that day and June 30, 2010. He urged the Legislature to take immediate action to rebalance the budget. Because the state had drained its bank account, the state simply did not have the cash to pay employees and vendors beginning in February 2009. Mac Taylor, the state's legislative analyst, put the accumulated deficit into perspective by saying that if the Legislature were to try to cut the budget by $28 billion in 2009–10, it would have to eliminate the entire budgets for higher education and social services programs, cuts most would think both extreme and unreasonable. The state treasurer, Bill Lockyer, pointedly admonished legislators: Until they addressed the state's budget problem, he could not issue the kind of debt necessary to keep infrastructure projects going. State capital projects, like road construction, would stop in February. The state's ailing economy would get weaker. Then, the day after the joint session, the governor told the press that the Department of Finance had reestimated revenues at $3 billion lower than had originally been thought. Standard and Poor's, a credit rating agency, downgraded the state to its lowest rating. In December 2008, the state's fiscal condition seemed to have gone from chronic to terminal.

Previous chapters described the components of the state's fiscal structure: revenue streams, expenditure patterns, and debt commitments. The deficit, as highlighted before that wintry joint session, is the net effect of the streams, patterns, and commitments. The deficit opened up before the economic slowdown that became evident in mid-2008 and is likely to persist after the state's economy recovers. This chapter describes how the state developed a large and ongoing permanent deficit.

Emergence of an Ongoing Deficit

In the spring of 2000, Assembly Speaker Bob Hertzberg wanted to change the way the Assembly conducted budget negotiations. Before becoming speaker, Hertzberg had watched the Assembly struggle to cope with the effect of a highly charged partisan environment. He noted that the Senate was able to either minimize or better direct the partisan differences in its house. The Senate could do this in part because it had a smaller membership and tended to be "clubbier." It also seemed to have more experienced members, as termed-out Assemblymembers tended to run for and be elected to the Senate. But Hertzberg noted that by managing its partisan conflicts better, the Senate seemed to improve its negotiating position over the Assembly. Repeatedly, the Senate would pass a budget with votes by Democratic and Republican senators, then adjourn and wait for the fractious Assembly to secure the necessary votes to do the same. More often than not, by finishing first, the Senate seemed better able to set terms for the budget settlement.

The Senate's experience, size, and collegiality seemed to temper internal squabbling. As speaker, Hertzberg had no control over the experience or size of his house, but as its leader, he could set a tone for the Assembly negotiations. When Hertzberg became speaker in 2000, he wanted to change the tenor and dynamic of the budget negotiations and in this way improve the Assembly's bargaining position. If he could secure Republican votes for the Assembly version of the budget before starting negotiations with the governor and Senate leadership, then the Assembly would have a stronger role in shaping budget negotiations. So he sought to minimize partisan conflict within his house before negotiating with the Senate and the governor. On Friday, May 19, the Speaker met in a conference room at the Los Angeles airport with Assemblymember Scott Baugh, the Assembly Republican Floor Leader. What, he asked the Republican leader, would it take to secure sufficient Assembly Republicans for the Assembly version of the budget?

Baugh noted that the state General Fund had experienced a remarkable increase in personal income tax revenues since 1996. In those years, income tax revenues grew from $23.3 billion to $44.6 billion.[1] He said he noted that the Assembly version of the budget included major increases in spending. He doubted that any Republican leader could vote for such a budget, but with a few spending changes and a $3 billion permanent tax break, he thought that a few Republicans might be able to vote for the Assembly budget.

Hertzberg was amenable to the spending changes, but did not think he could agree to Baugh's large and permanent tax cut. He might be supportive of a $2.5 billion reduction, but the Speaker was especially troubled by Baugh's insistence on an ongoing reduction.

Baugh was concerned that the growth in revenue was attributable to a spectacular run derived from taxes on capital gains and stock options. In 1994, for example, Californians reported net capital gains of a little less than $8 billion. Five years later, they reported net gains of over $52 billion. This represented an average annual increase of 45 percent, a growth rate far greater than the economy in general. The state benefited from this growth because the gains were taxed as income and therefore subject to the state's personal income tax.

Never before in the state's history had capital gains been such a large part of the income tax base. Analysts were divided about what to make of this change. If taxpayers were reaping more gains because they were being compensated with stock options rather than higher salaries, then their investment income would make up a greater part of their taxable income. As long as this practice continued—and the stock market continued to appreciate—the state could expect to accrue revenues from $52 billion in net capital gains (as it did in 1999) rather than $8 billion (as it did in 1994).

Other analysts were concerned that the growth in capital gains was a reflection of enormous speculative investments. If the speculators were merely realizing their investment gains and getting out of the stock market, investment income would not represent a permanent increase in the income tax base. Still others were concerned that the investment income was temporary because it reflected gains from an overheated stock market. If the stock market cooled, they argued, then the income tax base would return to a level more like 1994 than 1999.

No one could tell for certain which part of each analyst's explanation was accurate. Hertzberg was not sure how much of the state's revenue boom was permanent, and he was leery of permanently reducing the tax base in the event the revenue from capital gains was a temporary windfall.

The leaders haggled for a couple hours without resolving their differences. But before they left the conference room at LAX, they had agreed on one essential point: The Assembly budget would include a $2.7 billion tax reduction. The leaders agreed to vote for the Assembly version of the budget with a major tax cut, but left open the question about whether the state could afford a permanent reduction.

Hertzberg's concern about the permanence of the state's revenue boom proved to be more than idle worry when revenues crashed a year later. The revenue boom was sustained through much of the 1990s, but was over by 2001. From

---

[1] Department of Finance, *Governor's Budget*, 2009 Schedule 3.

1996–97 until 1999–2000, state General Fund revenues grew by an annual average rate of 13.4 percent. Expenditures grew at a healthy but slower pace, about 10.6 percent. When in 2001–02 revenues fell below their earlier levels, expenditure growth rates moderated. But expenditure levels did not fall as had revenues. Figure 6.1 compares revenues and expenditures for the period.

In retrospect, spending the revenue derived from taxes on capital gains seems thoughtless and heedlessly optimistic. But it was hard for the Legislature— Republicans and Democrats—and the governor to have anticipated the magnitude of the drop in revenues that occurred with the 2001 tax year. From 2000 to 2001, taxes on capital gains fell from $10.6 billion to $4.6 billion. The next year, taxpayers paid only $3.2 billion. Such large changes in capital gains were without precedent. Figure 6.1 displays the actual amounts of capital gains taxes paid, by tax year. It is unlikely in the foreseeable future that the state will accrue the same kind of revenue from capital gains that it did in 2000. What is so vivid now, nine years after the investment bubble burst, was not apparent to most observers in early 2002. As described in Figure 6.1's trend line, for the 11-year period starting in 1999, capital gains seem to be falling by at an average annual rate of between 5.0 percent and 6.0 percent. During the revenue run-up, the Legislature spent less than it took in and ran billion-dollar budget surpluses. Even so, it increased the state's "baseline" spending by enhancing existing programs and adding new programs. According to the Legislative Analyst's Office,[2] from 1998–99 to 2002–03 total General Fund expenditures increased by nearly $20 billion, increasing on average by more than 20 percent annually. Most of this increase, about $11.1 billion, financed the costs of higher prices (inflation) and caseload for existing programs. That is, over 55 percent of the increase in spending merely allowed departments to continue providing services at the levels they had provided in 1998.

Most of the other increased spending, about $8 billion, financed expanded or new services. The single largest increase in spending backfilled local governments for their loss of vehicle license revenue. This amount, about $3.7 billion, could be said to finance the cost of holding local governments harmless for the Legislature's vote to reduce taxes. K-14 schools received about $2.6 billion for new and expanded programs. Higher education received about $375 million more, primarily for enhanced financial aid. Medi-Cal programs increased by $1 billion. The Medi-Cal increases expanded health care to the working poor through the Healthy Families Program and provided for other expansions in eligibility.

After the Fall

The governor and Legislature continued to spend at high levels through the 2001–02 budget. Though the tax payments on capital gains fell dramatically for the 2001 tax year, taxpayers would not file their tax returns until April 15, 2002,

---

[2] Legislative Analyst's Office, "Sources of Spending Growth in Major State Programs." (Sacramento, Calif.: Legislative Analyst's Office), July 16, 2003.

Figure 6.1. Income Tax Revenue Derived from Capital Gains—Assumes 9% Tax Rate, 1999–2009 (Dollars in Billions)

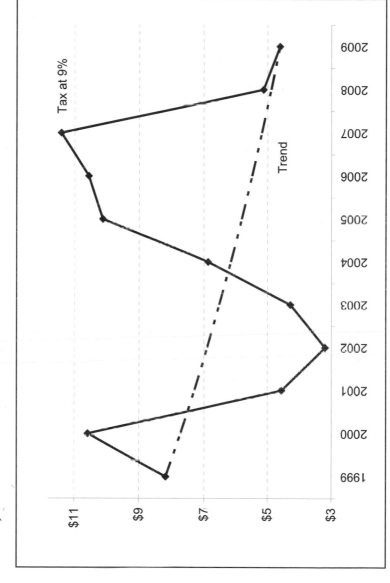

well after the 2001–02 budget was negotiated and signed. The governor and legislators did not have sufficient information about taxpayers' income to anticipate the sudden and precipitous drop in revenues until it was too late. Nor, for that matter, did the Department of Finance as it prepared the next budget in November 2001. As the governor introduced his budget in January 2002, the 2002–03 budget had been prepared assuming that capital gains might fall slightly, but not by the amounts that became apparent in April 2002.

Even after the magnitude of the budget problem became apparent, the state found it difficult to make permanent adjustments to the spending and revenue baseline established during the late 1990s.

In January 2003, Governor Davis proposed an $8 billion tax increase. This large increase, he said, would create a sustainable balance in the state's budget. His efforts, however, were overwhelmed by other statewide concerns. The state's electricity market eroded in dramatic and scary ways. The governor himself became subject to a bitter recall effort. And the Legislature resisted his efforts to balance the budget with a tax increase.

After his recall and Governor Schwarzenegger's inauguration, the state lost any chance of formulating a permanent response to the budget imbalance. In fact, Governor Schwarzenegger's first action as governor was to cut annual taxes by over $5 billion. During the Schwarzenegger years, the state continued to balance its annual accounts by reducing the expenditure structure, increasing debt, and developing ever-more complicated methods of deferring costs to out-year budgets. In the budgets since then, the state employed a variety of measures to provide temporary balance, but the budget maneuver has not significantly altered the state's fiscal structure. Indeed, California expenditures exceeded tax revenues in each year since 2000. To provide budget balance in each of those years, the state adopted a variety of temporary fixes. The state's fiscal problems became a harrowing, permanent imbalance. By 2008, as the national economy slowed and the state's economy followed, "Armageddon" had come to the state's budget, according to the governor.

The Problem Continues, Even After Economic "Recovery"

When the budget first developed its problems in the wake of the capital gains bust, many commentators expected the state's budget to recover with the economy. The state, they said, would "grow its way into balance." In hindsight, it is clear these commentators were wrong. After the joint session in December 2008, the media focused on the state's slide into recession. To be sure, as the economy slowed, sales tax receipts fell dramatically. Income tax receipts were expected to fall in 2008–09 as industrial output slowed and unemployment rose. Costs for state programs that respond to economic changes, such as unemployment insurance payouts, increased. But the deficits discussed in the context of the 2008–09 budget were merely exacerbated by, not caused by, the recession.

Even before the recession gave the governor apocalyptic visions, state treas-urer Bill Lockyer documented that the state's tax structure could not support the ongoing spending commitments. The existing fiscal structure, even assuming a "full employment" economy, likely would remain in perpetual imbalance by about four percent per year over 20 years.

On October 1, 2007, Lockyer offered a 20-year budget estimate of the state's General Fund condition.[3] The treasurer estimated that the income tax will grow from $58.6 billion in 2008–09 to $148.9 billion in 2027–28, growing at an average annual rate of 4.8 percent. During the same period, both the sales tax and corpora-tion tax were projected to grow at an annual average rate of about four percent. Sales tax revenue will grow from $31.4 billion to $71.6 billion, while the corpora-tion tax will grow from $10.6 billion to $22.6 billion. All other taxes will grow from $5.4 billion to $10.6 billion, at an average annual growth rate of about 3.4 percent. Total General Fund revenues will grow from $107.1 billion in 2008–09 to $248.2 billion in 2027–28. That represents an overall average annual growth rate of about 4.4 percent. For purposes of this base-case estimate, the treasurer's report made no attempt to model the business cycle. The estimates, therefore, represent a trend for the total growth in General Fund revenues.

To estimate the first four years of the operating budget, the treasurer relied on the legislative analyst's fiscal outlook for the period 2007–08 through 2011–12 for all but one small program. In the case of annuitant health benefits, sometimes re-ferred to as "other postemployment benefits," (OPEB) the treasurer made an esti-mate based on a 2007 actuarial study conducted by the state controller. The state typically finances annuitant benefits on a current—or "pay-as-you-go"—basis. The state controller identified both the cost for paying the accrued unfunded liabil-ity and the "normal cost" of funding the costs on the same manner as pensions (called prefunding). For purposes of making its 20-year estimate, the treasurer's office assumed the state will both fund "normal costs" and will finance the identi-fied unfunded liability over a 30-year period beginning in 2008–09. It further as-sumed that the state General Fund will finance 75 percent of the identified annui-tant costs (with special funds paying the balance).

For the remaining 16 years of the forecast, the treasurer made several assump-tions about programmatic growth. In particular, the state constitution establishes a funding minimum for the portion of the budget associated with kindergarten through high school and community colleges (K-14). While the Legislature can choose to fund schools above the minimum, the treasurer assumed that the Legis-lature will not exercise that discretion. For purposes of the entire period beyond 2011–12, the treasurer calculated the schools' funding levels using the formula known as "Test 1," which provides schools a fixed percentage of the state's Gen-eral Fund. For higher education, including student aid, the report assumed growth at the same rate as the combined rate of wage inflation and population. The treas-

---

[3] Bill Lockyer, *Looking Beyond the "Investment Planning for the 21ˢᵗ Century*, 2007 (Sacramento, Calif.), 13.

urer estimated education expenditures will grow from $49.2 billion in 2007–08 to $110.5 billion in 2027–28.

Medi-Cal is by far the largest component of the state's health budget. To estimate the growth in Medi-Cal expenditures, the treasurer assumed that costs would grow with the changes in population and with the medical inflation assumed by the controller's actuaries. The treasurer assumed the rest of the health budget—including dependent care, mental health, and drug and alcohol programs —would grow with wage inflation and population changes. The total health budget will grow from $20.4 billion in 2007–08 to $64.6 billion in 2027–28.

The treasurer expected social services expenditures to grow from $10.1 billion to $24.7 billion over the 20-year period. Criminal justice will grow at the same rate, from $11.3 billion to $26.2 billion.

For the balance of the budget, Lockyer included estimates of constitutionally required transfers from the General Fund to transportation programs, employee compensation, and the rest of state government (including resources programs, the tax agencies, and some state personnel costs). This category also includes constitutionally required transfers from the General Fund to the Budget Stabilization Account. Though special funds (tax proceeds from the sales tax on gasoline, for example) provide most of the support for transportation, the state constitution requires an annual transfer from the General Fund to transportation projects. Over the 20-year period, the treasurer expected this portion of the budget to grow at a rate commensurate with population changes and price inflation, from $1.6 billion to $3.6 billion.

The cost of the annuitants' health benefits is included in this "other" category, and rises from $1.2 billion to $4.6 billion. This amount is the estimate of the General Fund appropriation required to fund both full payment of the accrued unfunded liability and the normal cost. For the balance of this part of the budget, the treasurer assumed spending will grow at the same rate as wage inflation and population changes. In total, the "other" category will grow from $9.3 billion in 2007– 08 to $24.1 billion in 2027–28.

According to the treasurer, by 2027–28, the state's General Fund balance sheet will show a gap of $14.6 billion between the amount needed to pay debt service and the amount of General Fund revenues available after paying for operating expenditures. Put another way, the state will face a $14.6 billion shortfall between General Fund revenues and the needed funds to pay for both debt service and operating expenditures.

Budgeting Objectives

How should the state's continual deficits be understood? Budgetary "balance" is just one of many objectives the Legislature and governor pursue as they negotiate the annual budget.

As discussed in Chapter 5, "balance" is a comforting principle for organizing budget decisions, but it may not be necessary to achieve that goal in every year.

For example, for those budgets making extraordinary investments beneficial to future taxpayers, some of the cost for that investment can be responsibly deferred to the later beneficiaries. When the state faces an economic downturn and a sudden drop in revenues, it may be appropriate to rollover a piece of the deficit to cushion the programmatic effects of a recession. In addition, given the complex and elastic nature of the state's programs and financing streams there may be a practical constraint on achieving annual balance. Budgets may be constructed to achieve several fiscal and policy objectives that may not be mutually compatible or consistent following. The Legislature may wish to pursue the following alternative objectives as it constructs the budget.

- *Rigidity to limit spending.* In recent years, Californians repeatedly sought ways to limit the growth of government. These limits, indexed to measures such as population or per capita gross domestic product, are intended to constrain government spending to a specific share of affordability. By capping government expenditures, these efforts allow programmatic growth for some programs as other programs are downsized.

- *Control and transparency of budgets.* The budget allocates revenues collected from the public. The funds are held in a kind of public trust. Taxpayers and citizens expect the Legislature and governor to allocate funds with a clear and understandable rationale for how these funds are used. The public expects the Legislature to facilitate a review of the budget decisions by providing adequate accounting and by exercising fiduciary controls. In an age of broadly distributed information, the standards for this kind of timely and clear accessibility are high.

- *Efficiency and effectiveness of allocations.* Budgets can inspire public confidence in the efficiency and effectiveness of budget allocations. Though it may not be possible to ensure that the last budgeted dollar is allocated to its highest and best use, the public expects prudent spending. This objective is related to, but not the same as, control and transparency. It encourages a comparison of spending across budget categories. It answers the question: Which spending is the best use of available public funds?

- *Predictability, planning and sustainability of budgets.* Few budget appropriations are one-off allocations. For the continuing support for public assistance or operating departments, a particular budget year's allocations follow from expenditures made in prior years. They also imply a certain continuing commitment and support for the program in subsequent budgets. Even so-called one-time appropriations for capital improvements are made as part of a series of prior appropriations—a road system takes years to complete, for example. A one-time appropriation to build a state office building implies ongoing support for the departments housed in the structure. In these circumstances, the allocations in the annual budget reflect prior spending decisions and imply continued support. To fulfill this objective, the Legislature looks beyond a single year to ensure that the revenue stream can sustain the spending commitments.

- *Flexibility*. Budgets reflect changing economic and political conditions. The "affordability"—even "prudence"—of any particular budget depends on external factors, such as changes in the state's revenue patterns and evolving political considerations. The recall of Governor Davis and election of Governor Schwarzenegger were seen as indicators that the public wanted the car tax to remain low. This tax cut implied a $5 billion cut in state spending. The flexibility norm encourages the Legislature to adjust spending with changes to conditions internal and external to the budget.

Conclusion

In practice, the Legislature pursues several objectives when negotiating the budget. Taken together, these objectives reflect the broad array of expectations for the state spending. Given their breadth, their simultaneous achievement is unlikely. Indeed, some of these objectives may be competitive. A budget prepared to fulfill the objective of "flexibility" in the face of an economic downturn will tend to be less "predictable." A budget that meets the objective of "rigidity" may be less efficient than one prepared to ensure cost effectiveness. As all objectives cannot be met equally and simultaneously, the pursuit of one usually comes at the expense of the others.

As the Legislature, the governor, and California's citizens struggle to reshape and reform both the content and process of the budget, they may ask what sorts of budgeting objectives should be pursued? Which should have higher priority? And how should their achievement be evaluated?

The state constitution vests the Legislature with the power to appropriate funds and impose taxes, while the governor has broad authority to manage state fiscal affairs. If budgets are to change, the Legislature must provide the means and the method. No other state institution has the authority or the responsibility.

If the Legislature were to acknowledge that it replaced the singular objective of balance with a more nuanced set of objectives, it may find a different way to talk about the budget and to measure the state's fiscal performance. After considering its options, the Legislature may find that these alternative principles are even more difficult to implement than trying to balance the budget within any particular year.

Chapter 7

What Can Be Done?

Though legislators devote considerable time and effort to reviewing the governor's proposals and the state's fiscal condition, the Legislature misdirects its efforts on the budget bill, neglecting the fiscal effects of policymaking and emphasizing short-term fiscal goals. The Legislature can better use its ample fiscal authority.

The Legislature's fiscal powers derive from the authority granted in the state constitution, through which the Legislature retains sole authority to appropriate. But, because the constitution does not *require* the Legislature to appropriate, its fiscal authority is exercised both when it makes and withholds an appropriation. How it organizes itself, conducts the review, and negotiates the differences matters. The Legislature can improve the state's fiscal structure when it better manages fiscal complexity and increases its capacity to develop and negotiate a budget.

Manage Complexity

Given the complexity of the fiscal environment, a cursory analysis or under-developed proposal will rarely serve the Legislature's interests. Fiscal problems cannot often be fixed by adding or subtracting from an appropriation. Rather, to make a substantial improvement in the way a program functions or the success of its operations, the program must receive better management or revised operating instructions. To make programmatic improvements, the Legislature must acknowledge and understand both how the program is administered and its funding requirements.

Preceding chapters discussed the difficulty in evaluating individual appropriations against competing fiscal and political needs. In addition, as the Legislature attempts to manage several budget objectives beyond annual balance, the choices become increasingly conflicted.

Complexity is compounded as the Legislature attempts to more fully delineate the programmatic responsibilities of state and local governments and to integrate the administration of their shared responsibilities. But when the state stretches the use of state and local revenues, these shared programs become even more precariously financed. Programs become more difficult to manage as the Legislature attempts to limit program participation and leverage federal funds. Over time, when the Legislature revises program requirements and program administration, it often makes local management and oversight more difficult.

Changes in state-only revenues have further complicated state finances. The Legislature and statewide ballots have earmarked state-only taxes or newly levied fees to segregate revenue streams for specific programs. For example, in a statewide election in 2004, the voters approved a proposition to impose an income tax surcharge on the state's wealthiest taxpayers. The proposition directed the revenue to a special fund for the support of local mental health programs, rather than the state's General Fund. The proposition therefore shifted state-administered tax revenue from state purposes to local purposes. Earmarking like this means that funds have been circumscribed in their use, requiring better methods for tracking the revenue streams. It requires decision-makers to have a more detailed understanding about the limited use of earmarked revenues. It also creates challenges for the Legislature, which must use the funds for these limited purposes while trying to ensure that all programs are fully funded.

As a piece of legislation strictly limited to making appropriations, the budget bill has a limited scope. Through it, the Legislature and governor provide only broad direction about how the appropriated funds can be spent. The bill lists each entity receiving an appropriation and reflects spending for a single year.

Though it serves as a spending plan covering a 12-month period, it is not a substitute for long-term planning. For the same reason, it is not intended to be an investment plan. The bill's inherently shorter timeframe can affect the kind of decisions made.

For example, as discussed in Chapter 5, the Legislature and the governor can use the 12-month scope of the budget to shift costs beyond the 12 months covered in the budget bill. The Legislature can "balance" this year's budget by using revenues from next year. It can adjust budget accounting to "recognize" this year's costs in next year's budget. In this way, the 12-month budget bill creates incentives to make short-term decisions whose out-year consequences are discounted.

Even as these limits help the Legislature expedite its budget decisions, the rules are criticized for facilitating budget resolutions that produce expedient decisions rather than providing more substantial fiscal review. There is a tension, never fully resolved in the state's budget process, between completing the budget negotiations on a timely basis and making prudent budget decisions.

Chapter 2 described why the budget bill is a weak tool for making policy. On occasion in recent years, the governor and the legislative leadership have announced goals for the budget negotiations that are far outside the reaches of the budget bill. Whether the goals are reforms of the workers' compensation laws or authorization of various bond proposals, they attempt to use the budget negotiations to achieve legislative goals outside the parameters of the annual budget bill.

On other occasions, there have been attempts to use the budget for changing the management of departments and programs. Typically, these attempts fall far short because the budget process provides a poor handle on management and policy.

These initiatives typically attempt to use the urgency of completing the budget to achieve nonbudgetary goals, but invariably these nonbudgetary initiatives are half-realized as part of the budget negotiations. Rather than impose weak and nonbudgetary initiatives on the budget negotiations, the Legislature should concentrate its efforts on achieving closure on the budget. This means denying the governor's nonbudgetary goals, too. By doing this, the Legislature will focus the budget negotiations on those issues directly related to the budget bill.

The complexity and tenuous nature of budget decisions is magnified as budget stress encourages the adoption of short-term and expedient solutions. This complexity can be better managed in two ways.

1. Strengthen Fiscal Management Mechanisms

Because it merely authorizes spending levels, the budget bill cannot effectively or directly measure or predict consequences of funding levels. When the Legislature attempts to make broad policy changes through trailer bills, or when it tries to dictate specific management outcomes through appropriations, it will diminish its effectiveness.

2. Strengthen the Policy and Appropriations Committees

A way of enhancing the Legislature's ability to make policy is to strengthen the role and prerogatives of policy committees, especially relative to the budget committee. This can be done by ensuring that the budget process does not set new policy, especially policy that limits or repeals statutory law previously passed through the policy committees.

Another way to strengthen policy committees in the budget process is to refer all trailer bills to the policy committees.

What should be the role of the Appropriations Committee in each house? Each year, the Appropriations Committees pass bills that, if implemented, would raise annual state costs by billions of dollars. If the Legislature is going to assert its fiscal responsibilities, it may want to use the Appropriations Committees to limit programmatic changes approved in policy committee. The Appropriations Committees should be charged with ensuring that program changes approved in the committee can be sustained either with a new revenue stream or within the existing revenue structure.

Improve the Legislature's Capacity to Develop and Negotiate a Budget

As described in Chapters 1 and 2, the budget process is intended to move the negotiated parties to consensus, even as rivalries and institutional differences can create bitter disputes. The Legislature's fiscal authority is enhanced when it can better channel differences into negotiated resolutions.

1. Ensure Sufficient Information Is Available to Focus on Long Term

The most pervasive difficulty in the current process is the state's inability to look beyond a single fiscal year when crafting the budget. There is good reason for that. Cost and revenue estimates become more uncertain over time as years are added to the funding horizon. The Legislature can do much to improve its decision making. It can beef up its estimate capacity, identify costs in the later budget, and improve its response to downward trends in the General Fund condition.

2. Establish Budget Priorities Independently of the Governor's Budget Proposal to Afford the Legislature Greater Fiscal Independence

As long as the Legislature affords the governor the first draft of a budget, all its activities on the budget will be in response to the governor's January proposal.

All legislative changes will be compared to the governor's proposal. By allowing the governor to have the first draft, the Legislature limits its discretion. There are many ways the Legislature could counter the mesmerizing power of the governor's January proposal. The most direct way is to identify its financial and financing issues before release of the January 10 budget proposal.

With this in mind, the Legislature should begin negotiation on the budget before the governor makes his decisions in mid-December. The legislative analyst's office, after all, provides the Legislature with a fiscal update in mid-November.

Is it practical to expect that the Legislature could write its own budget? Since the governor has many more employees who can construct the necessary budget documentation and financial schedules, is it reasonable to expect the Legislature—

with a much smaller staff—to do the technical work necessary to develop its own budget proposal?

While it is undoubtedly true that the executive staff would continue to prepare the financial schedules, it is not clear that the Legislature cannot develop its own funding priorities, independent of the governor.

3. Consult with the Governor Prior to the Release of the January Budget

The legislative analyst publishes a forecast of the state's budget condition in mid-November. This forecast provides the Legislature with an assessment of the state's General Fund condition and identifies fiscal opportunities and threats. Between the time this forecast is released and the governor's State-of-the-State address, there is sufficient time for legislators to identify their fiscal priorities and convey them to the governor. In December—before the governor publishes the budget proposal—legislative leadership could provide the governor with its priorities in December. Another option is to use the Joint Legislative Budget Committee, which is empowered to act on fiscal matters when the full Legislature is not in session and which often corresponds with the governor when the Legislature is not meeting. The chair of the committee could identify in writing the Legislature's priorities for the next budget.

4. Truncate Subcommittee Review

Separately, each house spends five months developing a response to the governor's January budget. It uses the subcommittees from January through the end of May to take testimony, consider alternatives, and prepare a response to the governor's budget. These deliberations tend to be one-sided affairs. The subcommittees' agendas and actions tend to reflect the perspective and wishes of the majority party. The minority has little access to planning the hearing or contributing to the hearing agenda. At the hearings, the minority members rarely propose changes to the budget. All subcommittee actions are taken with a majority vote. In practice, this means that the Republicans vote as a bloc against the majority and do not influence the outcome of the subcommittee.

As a result, subcommittee work does not lead to furthering the necessary collaboration. It barely furthers the development of the budget.

Though the Department of Finance and representatives of the departments participate in subcommittee hearings, they are unable to engage the Legislature on alternatives to the governor's January budget proposal. Though there is some inter-house communication, there is little formal coordination between the houses around the budget. As a result, the work done in subcommittees reflects the singular perspective of the majority in each house. Only in the budget conference committee—after the subcommittees have completed their work and the governor has proposed a May Revision—will negotiations begin between the governor and the four legislative caucuses. The conference committee typically starts in June. As the budget is supposed to be completed no later than July 1, the subcommittees could be seen as delaying the beginning of negotiations. If the Legislature limited the work of each house's subcommittees, it could move more quickly into the inter-house bipartisan conference committee. This conference forum facilitates more collaborative consideration.

5. Move the Start of the Fiscal Year to October 1

Moving the start of the fiscal year will afford more time to review the relevant budget. When the Legislature receives the May Revision, it has roughly seven weeks to complete its review of the revisions and negotiate the entire budget before the start of the new fiscal year. If the governor proposes major changes, the Legislature is unable to give these new proposals the kind of consideration it gave the January proposal.

To give itself more time to review the May budget revision and formulate a response, the Legislature should alter the state's fiscal calendar to begin the fiscal year on October 1, like the federal fiscal year. The Legislature needs to avoid the jam it gets into following the May Revision. This extra three months would allow for greater consideration of the consequences of any spending or revenue change.

The delay would afford the Legislature sufficient time to develop an alternative to the governor's May Revision, and would give the Legislature greater control over the final budget product. Rather than defer to the May Revision, the Legislature would have time to develop an alternative.

Procedurally, the change would require the Legislature to stay in session through October 1 if it was unable to complete the budget before the start of the fiscal year.

To make this change in the budget calendar would be no small accomplishment. While the constitutional provisions requiring a July 1 start-date could be circumvented, if the Legislature were to pursue an annual fiscal year in conformity with federal law, it would be appropriate to seek voter approval for the constitutional change.

The change would also have some unexpected fiscal costs. If the Legislature were to change the start of the fiscal year to October 1, the first year of the new system would include a "transitional" budget for the quarter starting on July 1 and running through September 30.

The July-September quarter happens to be a low-revenue period. The state does not receive very much income or corporation tax revenue in the summer, so it is likely that the revenues generated during this "transitional" budget would be insufficient to cover expenses. These one-time costs could be as high as $2 billion.

6. Conduct a Postbudget Assessment and Review

Remarkably, for all the effort it invests in reviewing the governor's January budget proposal, the Legislature does rather little to monitor the implementation of the budget. Though the governor issues his January proposal with a well-articulated summary and the legislative analyst prepares a 300-page analysis of this proposal, there is very little analysis of the budget that is eventually adopted. Each budget committee publishes a brief review of the new budget and the legislative analyst distributes a 20-page highlights document, but the final budget never receives an analysis as painstaking as the initial proposal. Isn't that ironic? The governor's January proposal gets thorough commentary, but the completed budget gets virtually no analysis.

To improve its understanding of budget dynamics and ensure that its intent is administered, the Legislature should require a full analysis of the adopted budget. An analysis similar to the legislative analyst's review of the governor's proposal might be appropriate.

While not a complete solution, these changes—pretty major, all—would address specific concerns about how the Legislature manages the state's fiscal condition. Saying that the Legislature can act unilaterally does not imply that it can take these steps easily or with impunity. Implementing a more robust fiscal review may require a higher investment of institutional capital—so much so that the Legislature may conclude the current process and procedures are sufficient for achieving enough of its many institutional goals.

The procedural changes recommended above can offer the Legislature improved deliberations over the state's fiscal structure and help it better manage the broad consequences of fiscal action. Because the legislative process is a creature of the institution, the Legislature itself can take immediate steps to improve the way it creates and passes a budget. Change can come when a simple majority in either house agrees to them and will come when the institution itself decides it is in the house's "interest."

Procedural Change Is Not Enough

Procedural change is not magic, nevertheless. Procedural changes cannot, like some *deus ex machina* in an ancient play, resolve the contradictory and untidy bits of budget drama discussed throughout this book. Process, by itself, will not change the decisions made. The Legislature and governor have found myriad ways of subverting the constitutional, administrative, and statutory rules directing the budget. After all, the constitution prohibits the Legislature from assuming excessive General Fund debt, even as the state runs up billions of dollars of debt.

The solution to California's fiscal ills must come from within its institutions, not from externally contrived forces. If the Legislature is to better manage the state's fiscal environment, the inputs to its decisions—the very basis of its fiscal decisions—must change. The Legislature and governor must insist on receiving and publishing accurate information on the implications of its fiscal decisions, including:

1. What Are the Long-Term Outcomes and Trends of Prior Fiscal Decisions?

The Legislature must learn to see budget decisions in their longer context. Budgets, though annual in conception, have multi-year effects.

Each year, the governor and Legislature make fiscal decisions that extend well beyond the budget act itself. Establishing new entitlements create an expectation that those programs will continue in future years. Taxes, once reduced, are especially hard to increase. Capital investments, such as roads, have consequences beyond the budget year, as they affect the mobility and commutes of future drivers. Other investments in human capital, such as health and education programs, can affect the opportunities for future workers.

So too, California's economic and demographic conditions evolve over multiple years. The public trust suffers when the governor and Legislature ignore changing conditions and fail to prepare properly.

2. Who Is Served?

Budget allocations are not abstractions. They are made to programs, departments, and people. The governor and Legislature must make clear who receives the allocation and how that allocation is used. Most importantly, the budget allocations should provide a basis for measuring the successful use of public funds.

3. What Role Do Fees and Taxes Play?

The state's revenue structure does not exist in a vacuum. It serves the state by primarily financing programs for the public good. It may also serve to pursue social goals, including to transfer income and to impose incentives on certain types of activity. The governor and Legislature should pay particular attention to the role and effects of the revenue structure.

Build Consensus on Broad Fiscal Goals.

With this information, the Legislature can begin building broad acceptance among Californians for its fiscal decisions. In this regard, the two-thirds vote requirement for passing the budget helps build consensus. Because the budget cannot pass without a supermajority, the vote requirement imposes a partisan standard, requiring a broad coalition of support for any budget decision. As such, the reformers who call for a repeal of the two-thirds requirement may be encouraging quicker votes on the budget, but they may be simultaneously helping to diminish broad support.

Conclusion

Fiscal decisions have consequences. They can be powerful precisely because they fix a cost to each legislative choice. They help state leadership evaluate the myriad possible choices and assign them values: How much will it cost? Some of the procedural changes recommended in this chapter would require ratification of a constitutional change in a statewide election. Other revisions could be made by changing internal legislative rules and customs, changes that could be made with the assent of the membership of the houses.

As important as procedures are, however, the content of the budget and the attendant decisions are more important. Governing California is hard. Each economic cycle presents the Legislature with a challenge different from what that it faced in the previous cycle. Even within each year, the Legislature must evaluate, plan, and provide for the provision of present and future public services. Legislators face many conflicting demands on their time and talents. To follow the recommendations included in this chapter, each legislative house would have to engage time and political capital on the policy process. They would have to set and monitor substantive long-term goals for the management of programs. To be effective, the legislative institution will, of necessity, abandon some of its current pursuits in favor of concentrating on the state's fiscal policy and budget process.

Public polls and media reports suggest that the institution is in decline. By in vesting the time and capital in revising the processes and the kinds of decisions made, the Legislature can enhance its authority over the conduct of the state's business.

Because the budget is renegotiated every year, the Legislature must make decisions each year about not only current services, but must also prepare for the future.

The Legislature can improve the way it makes policy and financial decisions. It has the constitutional responsibility and the authority to make institutional and procedural reforms. The choices made in this new way will not necessarily be easier (indeed, the choices may become more complex and difficult). However, if the Legislature organizes to enhance its ability to wield this constitutional authority, it will enhance its power.

The state's current fiscal problems are the compounded effect of years of decisions. They reflect a breakdown in consensus about the size of government and the proper amount of governmental services. A more confident Legislature may be able to forge a consensus on broad fiscal objectives.